THE WITCHCRAFT HANDBOOK

THE WITCHCRAFT HANDBOOK

Unleash Your Magickal Powers to Create the Life You Want

MIDIA STAR

CONTENTS

INTRODUCTION

Welcome to *The Witchcraft Handbook*, where you will learn how to use magick to become stronger, happier and more in tune with yourself.

Witchcraft is the practical side of the Wiccan religion. This religion has been around since long before Christianity, and it bears little resemblance to most other religions followed today. For the pagans who introduced it, it was more a way of life than anything else. Wiccans worship, pray and give thanks to not just one god, but to the gods and goddesses of the entire universe, while respecting the views of other people's religions.

Witchcraft is about embracing life and trying to make the world a better place for everyone, no matter what their faith, religion, colour, creed or sex. It's a nature-based belief and we use the seasons, herbs, colours, candles, the moon and the sun to help with spells to attain our dreams and desires, and those of others.

In years gone by people would cast spells to help crops grow and protect friends and family from harm. Today we can use magick for similar ends, just updated for the modern world we live in. Magick can help you get the job you want, help you find and maintain a happy relationship, and even help out with your finances when you're broke. Witches are passionate about what they do, and generally get what they want out of life. They aren't sheep following the flock, and they believe that freedom of thought, respect of nature and kindness to other beings are more important than mindlessly adhering to so-called 'rules'.

This is why you need witchcraft in your life. It works on the basis that you have the power to choose everything you do with your life. If you do something that you know to be morally wrong, then you will have to accept the consequences of your actions. Likewise, when you use magick, you are wielding a real power. If you use it frivolously or to do harm or only for selfish means, you can bet it will come back to bite you.

We worship many gods and goddesses (we will talk about these later in the book) and in turn, these deities help us in our quest for a happy and fulfilling life. And by worship, I don't mean dropping to your knees and praying. The Goddess is all around us all the time. A mere word of thanks, or even just a 'good morning', makes the Goddess happy and, in return, she grants us what we need and desire.

Did you know?

You may be wondering why we don't spell magick the usual way (magic): this is simply to show that what we're doing has nothing to do with card tricks or pulling a rabbit out of a hat.

THE POWER
OF WOMEN

In the pagan Europe of thousands of years ago, every village had a 'wise woman', also known as a shaman, priestess or woman of power. She was the local doctor, midwife, veterinarian and pharmacist all rolled into one and naturally held a position of great respect.

With the introduction of the Christian religion in Europe, pagans were persecuted for refusing to conform, and their beliefs were either subverted into Christian-friendly holidays or portrayed as devil worship – hence the excuse for the burning and torturing of witches as well as any woman or man who was unfortunate enough to be accused of being one.

Thankfully, times have changed and, to a large degree, most people accept others for who they are, regardless of what they believe in.

Modern witchcraft is about reclaiming the power that is natural to you as a badass woman. Pagans recognised the strong links women have to the energies of nature and the universe, but these traits have been degraded through thousands of years of male-dominated culture.

Witchcraft helps you to identify your own needs, strengths and weaknesses, and gives you the tools to do something about them, helping you to uncover your dreams and live your best life.

THE RULES OF
THE CRAFT

Thanks to movies, books and the media, witches have come to be portrayed as something they are not. *Harry Potter*, *Sabrina the Teenage Witch* and *Buffy the Vampire Slayer* are all fantastic viewing, but not what witchcraft is all about. Witches can't fly, become invisible, zap people into oblivion, or jump in and out of spell books.

WHAT DO I NEED?

In movies, witches have a host of 'magickal' tools of the trade, but these are not requirements to perform magick. It doesn't cost anything to be a witch. Witchcraft was and still is about using the power of nature to help you in whatever situation needs fixing. It's not about buying an assortment of items: these are just magick commercialism.

The only tools you will find in this book are simple information about the phases of the moon and ingredients that are particularly favourable in magick and can hasten the effect of a spell. These include herbs that are readily available in supermarkets and simple items such as candles, ribbons, feathers, wood and a range of natural materials.

Just like other people, witches come in all shapes and sizes and most look no different to you. My usual attire is jeans and a T-shirt and the only time I wear a black cloak and a pointy hat is if I'm going to a fancy-dress party. So, as you can see, witches are just like any other person, they simply have the special gift of having this power to call upon when the going gets tough.

TWO SIMPLE RULES

'I thought witchcraft was about free living, no rules, and so on...' I hear you say. Yes it is, but without learning the rules of witchcraft, you will be ill equipped to perform magick, which will result in spells not working or going wrong, or even hurting yourself or someone else in the process. But don't worry, there are two rules you have to remember:

The Threefold Law: Whatever you do in life, be it good or bad, will come back to you three times. In fact, it can often come back to you up to seven times. Put simply, this means that if you do something that you know in your heart is not right, at some point in your life you will be paid back for it. This isn't so much a 'rule' as a law of nature, so it's worth paying attention to!

The Wiccan Reed: You can do whatever you like in your life, so long as you don't hurt anyone or anything. Again, think about the consequences of your actions prior to carrying them out. If you're going to be a true witch and true to yourself, think about other people's feelings before you fly off the handle and do or say something that will hurt them, however much they deserve it. Remember the Threefold Law: whoever hurts you will be paid back three times, so there's no need to take matters into your own hands.

HOW MAGICK CAN HELP YOU

Practical magick helps you to attain your goals and make your dreams a reality. The wonderful thing about magick is that you don't have to devote your entire life to it. The magickal skills you learn will always be there to call upon when you're down, need to find peace or have a problem that needs solving. Magick works hand in hand with your belief system. If you believe strongly enough that you can do something then there is nothing and no one that can stop you from achieving it. Your magickal powers will grow in tandem with your belief in yourself, and vice versa.

Although in this book I advise you how best to do a spell, you don't have to perform a ritual in any specific way. You don't have to set up an altar if you don't want to or you can't. Some witchcraft books will tell you a list of must-haves and must-dos. These 'musts' are not necessary: many are just props. I guarantee that if you have the belief, a spell will work even if you don't have the right coloured candle or do a spell when the moon isn't quite right. The moon phases, candles, herbs and all the other requirements listed in any spell help set the tone for a spell, meaning that the magick may be able to work quicker, but they are not 'musts'. For any spell all you need is the belief that it will work and to have faith in yourself and your powers.

WHAT WITCHCRAFT WON'T DO

Witchcraft can't make someone do something they wouldn't normally do. So, for example, doing a love spell to get the guy down the road to ask you out will not work if he is not remotely interested in you in the first place. A love spell can only suggest. Trying to force someone to do something they have no inclination towards will never work and may result in disaster for you and the person you're trying to bewitch.

GODS AND GODDESSES

Remember I spoke earlier about there not being just one god but several? Although we say that we ask for help from the Goddess, it is widely believed that different gods and goddesses help us with different things in life. So, for example, if you were casting a spell to find love, you would seek help from Aphrodite, the goddess of love. If you were thinking of forming a band, you would call upon Apollo, the son of Zeus and god of musicians. All the gods and goddesses come from ancient times, many being Greek or Roman – but we don't mind mixing them up, and you might find the odd Egyptian god or Archangel in the mix too.

Hera: The wife of the god Zeus, and is associated with women, marriage and childbirth.

Hestia: A goddess of protection who grants wishes for the home.

The Muses: The nine daughters of Zeus and Hera are true girlie girls – would you believe ancient pictures show them dancing around their handbags! The muses are like sisters who will help you with any problem you have as a girl.

Isis: Known by different names, Isis is primarily known as the goddess of womankind. She is the goddess most female witches call upon for help.

Did you know?

When we finish a spell we say 'so mote it be'. This might sound a little strange, but it's just an old way of saying 'so must it be'. Like the tools and ingredients used in the spells, we don't have to say it this way – we don't have to say it at all – but these ritual words and items help us to achieve the mindset and tune our energies to make our wishes become reality.

HOW AND WHY DOES MAGICK WORK?

Good question! Without going into too much detail, it's a combination of things. Most of us use only a tiny percentage of the power within us. The magick in this book is known as sympathetic magick, which means using symbolic objects to get magickal results. When we believe in ourselves and call upon the power of nature and the universe to help us, our wishes come true for all the things we want in life – and yes, even the material things!

DON'T SHOUT ABOUT IT!

Okay, so once you've discovered that witchcraft actually works, you're happy and content in the knowledge that for any problem or situation you may face in life, you can simply cast a spell and make it all better. I know it's tempting to tell someone that the reason your life is looking so rosy is because of the spells you cast, but you are looking for trouble if you go shouting from the rooftops that you're a witch and can work magick. If your friends are genuinely interested, you can tell them that you practise magick, but don't go around telling everyone.

THE SPELLS

Now you know the basics of working with witchcraft, we can get on with the fun stuff – the spells! Please remember, though, that witchcraft isn't the easy solution to everything you want to improve. If you perform a spell without feeling or belief, or think that every time you have a problem you can simply magick it away, it won't work. The Goddess is there for you at any time, but she doesn't like to be misused. If you start casting spells for the sheer fun of it, she will trip you up by sending you a sign of some kind.

Spells work best when you have a real need for something in your life, so only cast a spell when it's for something really important.

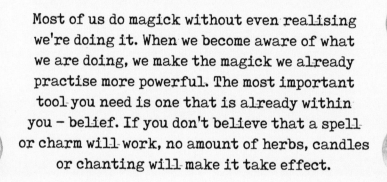

MAGICK MAKING

Most of us do magick without even realising we're doing it. When we become aware of what we are doing, we make the magick we already practise more powerful. The most important tool you need is one that is already within you – belief. If you don't believe that a spell or charm will work, no amount of herbs, candles or chanting will make it take effect.

THE MOON

The moon has long played a big part in our lives down here on Earth. Ancient civilisations worshipped it as a deity and measured the changing seasons by it. You will have noticed that, throughout the month, the moon seems to change shape. These changes are known as phases. There are eight phases that the moon travels through roughly every 29 days, which is how long it takes the moon to revolve around the Earth.

The moon affects the spells and magick we do. Although it is not necessary to perform a spell in a particular moon phase, it might help the magick to work quicker for you.

The eight phases of the lunar cycle are:
- The new moon: when the moon is not visible.
- The first waxing crescent: when the moon looks like a slim D shape.
- The first quarter: when the moon looks like a half circle in a D shape.
- The waxing gibbous moon: when the moon is egg-shaped.
- The full moon: when the moon looks like a basketball.
- The waning gibbous moon: when the moon is egg-shaped.
- The last quarter: when the moon looks like a half circle in a C shape.
- The waning crescent: when the moon looks like a slim C shape.

Here's an easy way to remember your magick-making moon rules: If you want something positive to happen in your life, do your spell on a full moon or a waxing moon. If you want something to disappear from your life, you should cast a spell on a waning moon.

CANDLES

Candles can play an important part in spell casting. The flame from a candle represents the element of fire and can be one of the most powerful vehicles to carry a wish into the universe. It doesn't matter if you can get only white candles because white is universal and will work happily with any spell. Different coloured candles for different kinds of spells are as follows:

- Red/pink: use for encouraging love, peace, harmony and everything slushy.
- Black/blue: use for banishing things you don't want in your life, such as an ex.
- Green: use for attracting money to pay that huge phone bill you've run up.
- Gold/orange: use these colours to enrich your life or career.

Always be careful when using candles. Put your candle in a candle holder, use safety matches or a lighter, and blow out the candle if you are leaving the room for any length of time.

1.

LOVE AND SEX SPELLS

This section is all about finding love and keeping it alive. When performing a spell for love, you need to be specific as to what you want – but we're not talking about trying to make a particular person fall in love with you. Everyone is entitled to his or her own free will, and if the person you've got your eye on isn't interested in you, trying to bewitch them is a dangerous game.

By 'specific' I mean stating what kind of relationship you are looking for. Before you cast a spell, think carefully about what it is that you really want (and, more importantly, what you don't want) in your love life. If you simply ask for lots of love and to be wanted and needed, you might find six adorable kittens on your doorstep one morning – lovely, but not quite what you were looking for!

MAGICKAL
PERSONAL AD

This spell is designed to attract love to you by
way of sending a personal advertisement into the
universe. Don't worry, for no one else will see this
spell, so you can really let your imagination go
wild and write down everything you want in your
ideal partner.

YOU WILL NEED:

A word processor
and printer

Or a pen and paper

Scissors

One pink candle

Matches or a lighter

WHAT YOU DO:

Do this spell on a full moon. You've doubtless
seen the personal ads at the back of newspapers
and magazines. You are now going to design your
own personal ad to send out to the universe – but
don't panic, you are not required actually to
send this to a newspaper or magazine, so you
can be as specific as you like!

Type out your 'wanted' ad and print it out,
or draw it by hand. You should make it personal
to yourself, but, as an example, mine might read
something like this:

Wanted!
A Prince Charming required to
Sweep this princess off her feet.
Must be kind, considerate and
Ready to fall in love.
Only genuine princes need apply.

Cut out your advert and place it under your pink candle. Light the candle. You can now sit back and relax. Let the universe take care of the rest and carry your wish to all those available.

Did you know?

The best days for practising relationship magick are: Tuesdays for spells to protect you; for example, to safeguard you from attracting the wrong person for you. Fridays for spells associated with love; for example, attracting Mr or Mrs Right. Saturdays for banishing something from your life, and Sundays for confidence and success, for example, if you need the confidence to ask out the person you like.

I WANT YOU

This spell is designed to attract an ideal partner. The ingredients listed below are chosen to represent everything you need for a good relationship, but feel free to choose your own symbols based on what is meaningful to you, and the qualities that are most important to you.

YOU WILL NEED:

One large horse chestnut leaf (for strength)

One ball of cotton wool (for softness)

One boiled sweet (tough on the outside, sweet on the inside)

One white feather (for kindness)

A piece of string

WHAT YOU DO:

Do this spell on a Friday night and a full moon. Find a quiet moment when you can relax in a nice warm bath. Place the horse-chestnut leaf in the bath water with you and, while you relax, imagine what your ideal partner will be like. Your visualisation will be transferred to the leaf. When you get out of the bath, wrap yourself in a big fluffy robe or towel. Lay the leaf on a hard surface (such as a dressing table) and place the cotton wool ball, the boiled sweet and the feather in the middle of the leaf. Fold the sides of the leaf up to the centre and tie your parcel with the string. Say, 'I want that man/woman!' Bury the parcel in the front of your garden or in a window box at the front of your house or apartment and wait for the magick to take effect.

SUMMONING YOUR
PERFECT MATE

This simple spell works on the principle that
if you tell the universe something long enough,
you create the power for that something to
become reality.

YOU WILL NEED:

Your own email
address
- -

WHAT YOU DO:

Do this spell on a Friday night. Open up your
e-mail and write yourself a message. The text
should read something like:

The one for you is on their way.

Type the message three times and send the email
to yourself. Don't open the message until the
next day. This allows time for it to travel
around the universe and silently inform all
out there that you are now available.

Repeat this action for the next three
Fridays. Continue to live life as normal, but
keep your eyes open! Because your message is
reaching the entire universe, you never know
when you might bump into your perfect mate.

ATTRACTING COMMITMENT

You may have no problem attracting someone,
but there comes a time in every woman's life when
she wants a bit of commitment – even if it's just
introducing you to their friends. This spell
will attract only those who will be true to you
and prepared to show it.

YOU WILL NEED:

A strip of paper

A tall glass of orange
juice

A handful of
seasonal berries
(strawberries,
raspberries and
so on)

One drop of rose oil

A blender

A romantic novel

WHAT YOU DO:

Do this spell on a waxing moon. Write the
following words on the strip of paper:

This man/woman I meet
will never stray

This man/woman I meet
won't run away.

This man/woman I meet
will be intimate

This man/woman I meet
will want to commit.

So mote it be.

Pour the orange juice, berries and rose oil into the blender, and blend for one minute. Pour the mixture into the tall glass. Dip the strip of paper into the glass and allow it to soak up some of the juice. Take it out again and place the strip on a sunny windowsill to dry. Drink your glass of juice. When the paper is dry, place it between the pages of your favourite romantic novel and wait for Mr or Mrs Commitment to come into your life.

Did you know?

Many beginners at spell-craft expect a spell to work immediately. Or they may hurry a spell to make its results come more quickly, but I'm afraid they will be disappointed. 'Patience' and 'practice' are two key words when making spells. It's not realistic to do an attraction spell for love and expect Mr or Mrs Right to appear on your doorstep in a puff of smoke. It takes time for your wish to travel to the universe and be granted. Most spells will work within one lunar month (29 days), though it might take a few months for you to reach your goal.

SUCCESSFUL
FIRST DATE

We all get the jitters when we're going on a
date with someone new. You know how it is: your
stomach is in knots and countless times you go
back to the mirror to check that you look okay.
This little spell will ensure that you have a
fun time on a first date.

YOU WILL NEED:

A red pen

A piece of white paper

One red rose petal

One piece of red
cotton thread or
ribbon

One rose incense stick

Matches or a lighter

WHAT YOU DO:

You can do this spell any time, in any place.
Write the name of the person you are going out
on a date with in red pen on the white paper, and
next to it write your own name. Place the red
rose petal on top of the names and then roll the
paper up into a scroll. Tie it with the red cotton
thread or ribbon. Next, light the incense stick
and pass the scroll of paper through the smoke.
Say the following three times:

Goddess of love
Make this date successful.
Goddess of love
Make this date one to remember.
Thank you, so mote it be.

Bury the scroll in the ground and enjoy your
date. It should go without a hitch!

ROSE QUARTZ ATTRACTION SPELL

Okay, I know I said you can't force someone to fall in love with you, but occasionally someone needs a hint that you are interested in them – remember, people are only human and after all, they're not mind readers! If you want to find out if someone is interested in you and want to send out signals that you're interested in them, try out this spell.

YOU WILL NEED:

One piece of rose quartz

WHAT YOU DO:

You can do this spell any time. Begin the spell by sleeping with the piece of rose quartz under your pillow one night. The following morning, hold the rose quartz in your dominant hand and close your eyes. Visualise your personality and all the good points about you being transferred to the rose quartz. Hold the quartz up in the air and imagine it sending out invisible signals to the person you are interested in.

Try to do this every day for a week, for ten minutes at a time. You should soon notice that the one you like has become interested in you and is beginning to look at you in a different way. You might even find that the magick has rubbed off on others, too!

LET THE RIGHT
ONE IN

There can come a time when you wonder if you're
destined to spend a lifetime picking the wrong
partner. This easy-to-make love charm wards off
unsuitable suitors, so that only the right ones
will come knocking.

YOU WILL NEED:

A black or grey pebble

A river

A white pebble

A 30 cm (12") length of
leather thong

WHAT YOU DO:

Do this spell on a full moon. Depending on
whether you are right- or left-handed, hold
the black or grey pebble in your less dominant
hand. Visualise all the unsuitable lovers who
have been in your life being absorbed into the
pebble. Think about the traits in them that were
unsuitable and transfer all of these into the
pebble. When you feel satisfied, open your hand
and say:

*Pebble, please take these unsuitable people
out of my life and stop me from attracting
them once and for all.*

Now take the black or grey pebble to a river or
pond and toss it over your shoulder into the
water. Don't look back at it.

When you get home, take the white pebble in your more dominant hand and visualise all the traits you would like to see in a partner. Think carefully about what it is that you require from them, and transfer all this energy into the white pebble. When you feel satisfied, take the piece of leather and wrap it around the pebble as many times as you can, tying it in a knot. Keep this charm with you at all times for at least 29 days. You will soon start attracting the kind of partner who is right for you.

MAKE ME
IRRESISTIBLE

We all like to look good when we go out, don't we?
This little beauty spell is not only easy to do,
but is designed so that you will look totally
kissable when you head out for the evening.

YOU WILL NEED:

One drop of vanilla
essence

Your best lipstick

WHAT YOU DO:

This spell works best on a full moon. Rub the
vanilla essence over the shaft of the lipstick
and allow it to dry. Just before you are due
to go out, carefully apply your lipstick and
visualise it being your ultimate attraction
weapon. Smack your lips together and say:

My lips are so kissable
They will make me irresistible
You will not be able to resist
The power of my kiss.

Now go out and knock 'em dead! I'm sure this
spell was designed for Cinderella, because it
only lasts for one night. But you can repeat
the ritual whenever you need it.

FLIRTATION
SPELL

We all have hang-ups that impair our self-esteem, and flirting with someone requires a certain degree of confidence. This spell will help boost your flirtation skills and make you feel more confident when you meet someone you're attracted to.

YOU WILL NEED:

One red candle

One pink candle

Matches or a lighter

A pinch of cinnamon

A plain envelope

One daisy chain

WHAT YOU DO:

Do this spell prior to going out for the evening. Light your candles, then run yourself a warm bath. Place the pinch of cinnamon in the bath with the daisy chain that you have made. Relax in the bath and visualise how confident you will be when you go out, and how your confidence will attract people from all over the place!

When you feel ready to do so, get out of the bath and get changed. Remember to blow out the candles. Fish the daisy chain out of the water, gently towel it dry, put it in the envelope to protect it, and take it out with you in your handbag. This is a very fast-working spell, and you should notice how quickly and easily you can flirt with someone you like, and how readily you attract people to you on your night out.

SPICY SEX LIFE

If you want to spice up your sex life, try making this delicious fruity drink for you and your partner to share. If you don't drink alcohol, you can do this spell using a bottle of fruit juice or non-alcoholic wine (readily available from most grocery stores).

Did you know?

The best candle colours to use in relationship magick are pink, red and gold. These colours are associated with love, intimacy and tranquility – all you need for a magickal relationship. If you need to do a banishing spell, a dark blue candle will work best.

YOU WILL NEED:

One bottle of red wine
or a fancy fruit juice

- -

A large saucepan

- -

Three drops of lemon
oil

- -

Three tablespoons
of sugar

- -

Five blackberries

- -

Three drops of
vanilla essence

- -

A piece of muslin or
a clean tea towel

- -

A large jug

- -

One pink candle

- -

Matches or a lighter

- -

WHAT YOU DO:

You can do this spell on any night of the week.
Pour the bottle of wine/juice into the saucepan.
Add the lemon oil, sugar, blackberries and
vanilla essence. Gently heat the mixture on
the stove and allow the ingredients to combine.
Allow the mixture to cool and then drain it
through a piece of muslin or a clean tea towel
into a large jug.

When your love arrives, pour the mixture
back into the bottle and light the pink candle.
Pour three glasses of magick wine – one for
yourself, one for your partner and one for the
goddess of love. Say the following just once:

> *This wine I drink with you tonight*
> *Our desire and passion will soon ignite.*

Relax and enjoy your evening together – it
should be one to remember...

RELIGHT MY FIRE

Juggling life and work can take up most of
our time – when we go to bed the only thing
we want to do is sleep. This spell will rekindle
lost passion.

YOU WILL NEED:

One acorn

Three pink candles

Five drops of lavender
oil

Five drops of rose oil

A bottle with a
spray attachment
(an old perfume bottle
will do)

----

120 ml (half a cup) of
natural spring water

WHAT YOU DO:

Take a warm bath and perform your spell.
Fill the bottle with spring water. Add the five
drops of each oil and shake. Place the candles
around your bedroom and spray each one with the
mixture. Also spray the bedsheets and the air
of the room.

When your partner arrives, light the candles
and say:

Goddess of love,
this is my desire.
Grant me my wish
and relight my fire!

Hold the acorn in your hand for a moment,
and then place it under your pillow when
you make love.

BREAK-UP WAKE-UP

Breaking up is hard to get over at the best of
times, but if you allow yourself to wallow over
it indefinitely, you'll prevent yourself from
meeting your true soulmate. This spell will help
you get over the pain. It is cast in two stages: the
first stage is to banish your heartache, and the
second is to send a message out there that you are
ready to go again.

YOU WILL NEED:

One dark blue candle
and candle holder

A handful of salt

Matches or a lighter

One pink candle

One crystal

WHAT YOU DO:

Do this spell on a Saturday when the moon is
waning. Take the blue candle and place it on
your window sill in the candle holder. Cup the
salt in your hand and pour a circle of it all
round the candle. Light the candle, close your
eyes and say:

The heartache I feel must go away
It does me no good to feel this way.
Take my heartache and set me free
So that I can find love again and be happy.

Allow the candle to burn down. Wait two hours, then take the pink candle and place it in the same candle holder. Put the crystal in front of the pink candle, then light the candle. Say:

I am now free to find love again.
Send this message to the universe
So that I may find true love
And keep true love.

Allow the pink candle to burn down completely, and place the crystal in your purse or handbag.

REUNITED
IN LOVE

Sometimes we lose touch with someone whom we
realise was our ideal partner. Although you
can't force someone to return to you, if you feel
that you were meant to be together you can try
this spell to seek them out again and rekindle
old passions. You never know – they might be
feeling exactly the same about you.

YOU WILL NEED:

Two pins

One white candle

A piece of paper

A pen

Matches or a lighter

WHAT YOU DO:

Do this spell on a full moon. The two pins
represent you and your old flame. Stick one pin
into one side of the candle and the other into
the opposite side. Write a message to the one you
loved, and their name, on the piece of paper and
place this under the candle.

Light the candle and say the name of the one
you wish to be reunited with 100 times. Allow the
candle to burn down and the pins to drop. This
signifies that your message has been received.
If you notice the flame sparking, you should
hear from them within a week. If you notice a
glowing ring as the candle burns, your wish
will be granted within 29 days.

THE NATURAL WITCH

Witches observe the power of nature; they have an intuitive connection with the energy that runs through the earth and universe, and a respect for every living thing. Perhaps you feel this too – do you live near the sea or water? Do you enjoy the mountains, have an affinity with animals or simply feel better for feeling the energy of the sun on your face in the warmer months?

THE FOUR ELEMENTS

Magick understands everything as having been created from the four energies of fire, air, water and earth, which represent the four points of the compass, the four quarters of the magickal circle and the four seasons. These energies form the universe and everything within it and are incredible sources of magick and energy. They each have their own strengths and weaknesses, powers and qualities.

Fire (the colours of reds, oranges and golds) represents light, heat, desire, fertility, passion, courage. We use it in candle magick by burning candles of particular colours for a certain number of days, burning pieces of paper to banish things from our life, or perhaps embracing the power of the sun. Its direction is south and its season is the summer.

Air (the colours of whites, blues, greens and yellows) represents mental acuity, knowledge, memory, friendship and reason. We use air magick in incense spells, through the power of the spoken word, through visualisation and mirror spells. Its direction is east and its season is the spring.

Water (the colours of blues, greys, greens and whites) represents our emotions, intuition, health, fertility. We use water magick through the use of the sea and shells, or through pools of water. Its direction is west and its season is the autumn.

Earth (the colours of browns, purples, greens and black) represents security, stability, strength, patience, warmth and cold, animals and the land. We use earth magick when we bring crystals or stones in our charms, herbs or plants, or when we bury something in the earth. Its direction is north and its season is winter.

BRING HARMONY TO YOUR LOVE

Arguing never solves anything – all it does is
sap your energy. This spell will put a halt to
the arguments and restore a happy, harmonious
atmosphere to your relationship.

YOU WILL NEED:

One onion

A knife

One blue candle

Matches or a lighter

One white candle

One white feather

WHAT YOU DO:

Do this spell on a Saturday night when the
moon is waning. Chop the onion into four equal
sections, then place one quarter in each corner
of your family room. Light the blue candle and
say three times:

> *Banish the arguments now*
> *Banish the hostility now*
> *Banish the hurt now*
> *So mote it be.*

Allow the blue candle to burn right down and
bury any remaining wax in your garden. Wait
for one hour, then light the white candle and
place the white feather next to it.

Now say three times:

Bring peace and harmony now
Bring love and excitement now
Bring happiness now
So mote it be.

Blow your wish carefully into the white feather. Allow the candle to burn down. Then take the feather outside and throw it up into the air, allowing it to be carried off into the universe.

Keep the onion quarters in your home for fourteen days.

A FOREVER TALISMAN

A talisman is a charmed piece of jewellery that attracts positive energy. It takes on properties that work as powerful magnets to attract and hold love. To bewitch your partner so that they will always have eyes for you, make this easy charm.

YOU WILL NEED:

A gold locket and a length of gold cord or a gold chain

- -

Three drops of lavender oil

- -

A photo of yourself and your loved one small enough to fit in the locket

- -

A small amount of lavender, basil and rosemary, chopped finely or ground up

- -

WHAT YOU DO:

Do this on a Friday during a waxing moon. Place the three drops of lavender oil on the locket and rub them in. Place the photo inside the locket, along with the chopped or ground herbs.

Hold the locket in your hands and visualise yourself and your partner being happy together forever. Say three times:

Our love is forever sealed within
  this talisman.
May a lifetime of happiness begin.

You don't always need to be wearing the talisman for the magick to keep working; it will just be stronger when the talisman is worn.

REMEMBER ME ALWAYS SPELL

You're special, right? To make sure your partner remembers that, and never forgets your birthday or anniversary, this spell will help keep their memory sharp.

YOU WILL NEED:

A calendar

A pad of Post-it notes

A red marker pen

A gold candle

WHAT YOU DO:

With the pen, mark on the calendar all the dates that are important to you, such as your birthday, the first time you met your love, your anniversary, and so on.

When you've gone through all the months on the calendar, write each important date on a separate Post-it note and stick them up where your partner will see them.

Light the gold candle and say once:

*You will remember what is important to me
From this day forwards and forevermore.
So mote it be.*

The message you send out to the universe will ensure that your partner never forgets those special dates. They may not even notice the visual reminders, but subconsciously they'll help them to know what is important to you.

RECAPTURING FIRST LOVE

Romance in long-term partnerships often has to take second place, particularly if you have other commitments that take up your time and energy. This spell will recapture those special moments when you first fell in love with your partner.

YOU WILL NEED:

A piece of paper

A red pen

A sample of your partner's handwriting (such as an old love letter)

One red candle

Matches or a lighter

WHAT YOU DO:

Do this spell on a Friday night. Write on the piece of paper all the things that made you fall in love with your partner in the first place. Think about the first time they chatted you up (or you them). Remember how your stomach flipped whenever you saw them or heard their voice? Then write down all you can remember about what first attracted him to you.

When you've finished, place the sample of your partner's handwriting face down on your piece of paper, so that the two lots of handwriting are pressed against each other. Put the red candle on top of the two pieces of paper and light it.

Say the following once:

Aphrodite, goddess of love
Send your magick to restore our love
Make us as we once were.
I send this message to you above
So mote it be.

Blow out the candle and relight it for the next seven nights. You should notice that your relationship with your partner becomes as magickal as it was when you first met.

THE (ANTI) ROMEO AND JULIET SPELL

It's not easy trying to maintain a happy relationship when your friends and family are against it right from the start. *Romeo and Juliet* was a great story, but you don't actually want to live it. So whatever it is that's making the people you care about have trouble accepting your loved one, this spell will banish any animosity, so that you are free to date whoever you wish to.

YOU WILL NEED:

One red candle

One blue candle

An item that represents you and your partner (a gift of jewellery that they have given you or a photograph of you together is ideal)

One teaspoon of mixed herbs

One teaspoon of salt

Matches or a lighter

WHAT YOU DO:

Do this spell on a waning moon. Place the red candle and blue candle next to each other. Put the item relating to you and your partner in front of the two candles. Place the herbs and salt on top of the item. Light the blue candle first, and say:

By the power of the goddess of love
I hereby ask you to banish the interference
* of others from our lives*
Let me be free to make my own choices in love.

Allow the blue candle to burn down. Then light the red candle, and say:

By the power of the goddess of love
Allow our love to conquer all
May we be happy for evermore.

Allow the red candle to burn down. Take the herb and salt mixture and throw it out of the window. Finish the spell by saying:

This is my wish, so mote it be.

MIRROR, MIRROR, ON THE WALL

Mirrors hold powerful magick within them, but
the trick is to know how to unleash it. This
spell will release the power of magick from a
mirror and send out signals to others that you
are interested in a relationship.

YOU WILL NEED:

A handful of silver
glitter

A handheld mirror

One white candle

Matches or a lighter

WHAT YOU DO:

Do this spell on a Friday. Perform this spell
when you have a spare half-hour to yourself.
Take a bath or a shower and cleanse yourself.
Be generous with the bubble bath or lotion and
make it a luxurious experience. Wrap yourself
in a towel, dry your hair and apply your makeup, as if you were going out on a big date. When
you feel at your best, sprinkle the silver
glitter all over the glass of the mirror, then
light the white candle and place it in front of
the mirror. Say the following words three times:

> *By the strike of three*
> *Let them see me*
> *And bring love rushing to me.*

Blow the glitter from the mirror and look
into it for a moment. See how vibrant you are!
Close your eyes and count to three. By now your
message will have been sent out to the universe.

GOODBYE WITH A SMILE

Sometimes we just know that a relationship isn't going to work out and it's best for all concerned to end it. Do this spell one week before you tell your partner – this should result in a happy parting.

YOU WILL NEED:

A Queen of Hearts playing card

A King of Hearts playing card

A pen

One black pebble

A pond or river

WHAT YOU DO:

Do this spell on a waning moon. Write your name on the Queen of Hearts playing card and your partner's name on the King of Hearts card. Lay the Queen of Hearts face up on a table, and place the black pebble on top of it. Now lay the King of Hearts face down on top of the stone. Hold your more dominant hand over this sandwich and say:

For us to move on
This time must end
We will both be free and happy
And remain good friends.

Fold the two cards in two and dispose of them (responsibly – witches don't litter!). Throw the black pebble into a pond or a river. You should now be able to part on good terms.

THE BOOK OF SHADOWS

A Book of Shadows is rather like a witch's diary, somewhere you record your spells, charms and witchy information, from noting the phases of the moon to favourite spells, and any notes about spellcasting that you find helpful as you develop your craft.

USING YOUR BOOK

Your Book of Shadows is your personal magick book, so take time to create something that is unique and meaningful to you. Choose a notebook that attracts you (probably something hardbacked with plain pages for you to add to as you need). Some shops sell leather-bound notebooks especially for this. Take the time to decorate it if you wish – you could use glitter, illustrations that appeal to you, or simply find a special pen to write in it with. The most important thing is that it feels right for you and that you will use it. Don't let anyone tell you that it has to be a certain colour or size – the only thing it should be is unique to you.

Once your book is ready, note down spells that you have had success with or want to try, or witch lore that you want to use in your magick. You could divide it into sections for different types of magick, or different times of the year. Treat it as you would a journal – make it useful for your spellcasting and what you are looking to change in your life. You could include pictures of things you want in your life, or try pressing the herbs and flowers you like to use in your magick.

MAKING YOUR OWN SPELLS

As you become more confident in your spell work, you will probably want to try making your own spells. Although I have tried to cover many eventualities in this book, when circumstances arise that call for a spell not provided here, you can easily design your own spells for your Book of Shadows.

Use the moon phases, candle colours and days of the week and other information listed in this book for the appropriate wish, then put together your own words to meet your particular situation. Spells don't necessarily have to rhyme – but they are easier to remember and more fun to chant if they do. Just be very clear about your intent for your spell.

2.

FRIENDS AND ENEMIES SPELLS

Everyone deserves to be treated fairly and surrounded by positive, supportive people. When you have someone in your life who makes you feel good about yourself, it's great to be able to give them something back through your magick.

If you sense that all is not as it should be in a friendship, take time to carefully consider the situation before embarking on your spell casting. Never do magick when you're angry, upset or just after an argument. Take time to calm down, think about the situation and consider all remedies before deciding what to do. When you perform the spell, be very sure about what outcome you are looking for and frame your spell with clear intent.

Just as with love spells, be careful when casting spells on friends and enemies, remembering the threefold law and keeping positive intentions in your heart.

MAKING FRIENDS

Some people can make friends just like that, but for others it's not so easy. You might be shy or worried about making the first move. You might have had to move away from your home town, or you've just started a new job. This spell will help you to make and keep new friends.

YOU WILL NEED:

A blank postcard

A gold pen

A bay leaf

Clear adhesive tape

A 30 cm (12") length of thin gold ribbon

WHAT YOU DO:

Do this spell on a Sunday or a Wednesday, or on a new or full moon. The postcard is to write your request for new friends to enter your life. Take the gold pen and at the top write the word WANTED, then underline it. Now write what kind of friends you would like in your life. You could write something like:

WANTED
Fun and caring friends at work/school/home
Who like me for who I am.
New friends who I can confide in,
Go out with and enjoy myself with.

When you've done this, stick the bay leaf to the postcard. Carefully roll up the postcard into a tube shape and tie the gold ribbon around it.

Leave the scroll on your bedroom windowsill for 24 hours so that your message will be carried to the universe, then place the scroll somewhere in your bedroom. You should soon see new friends entering your life.

MAKING-UP SPELL

We can all get a bit hot-headed from time to time
and say things we don't really mean. This spell
will reverse the insults you and your partner or
friend have exchanged when you've had one of those
almighty rows and have maybe come out with some
things you wish you hadn't. If saying sorry doesn't
cut it, try this reversal spell instead.

YOU WILL NEED:

A handful of salt

A small handheld
mirror

WHAT YOU DO:

Do this spell on a new moon. First of all, find
an area where you can sit undisturbed for ten
minutes. Cast a circle of salt around you and
the mirror. Look into the mirror and try to look
past your own reflection. Your eyes might glaze
over and water – this just means you're doing it
correctly. Say the following:

> *Mirror, mirror, in my hand*
> *Please listen to my command*
> *By the power of thoughts inside my head*
> *Take back all the awful things we said.*

Repeat this five times, then turn the mirror so
that you can no longer see yourself in it. The
reversal spell is now complete, and you and the
other person will be able to move on as though
it never happened.

LOOK AFTER
YOUR FRIENDS

Your friends may not be into witchcraft, but that doesn't
mean you can't help them with a little practical magick
when they're going through a rough patch. The only
provision when casting a spell for someone else is that
you do get their permission. You don't have to say, 'Look,
I'm a witch and I can cast a spell to make it all better for
you.' The mere fact that your friend has confided in you is
a cry for help. Ask if they would like you to try to help.
If they ask how you can possibly do anything, simply say
you'll do what you can. You will find over time that if and
when your friends discover your magickal powers, they
will automatically come to you to fix their problems. This
is fine, but just make sure that it's a problem that they
really need help with and that they're not just being lazy.

Silver glitter

Some soft modelling clay

A bay leaf

One white tealight candle

Matches or a lighter

Cast this spell on any day during any moon phase. Place some silver glitter in your hands and then roll the soft modelling clay between your hands. As you do this think of your friend's problem. It could be that she has relationship troubles; parent problems; school problems. Whatever the issue is, concentrate on the words she used to tell you about her problem. Next, create a little person out of the glittery modelling clay – this is going to represent your friend.

Put your model on top of the bay leaf. Place them both behind the white tealight candle and light the candle. Say the following words:

Goddess Athena, please help me to help [name]
May you take on this problem
To bring her comfort and healing
So that her problems will fade away
May her worries be gone
And her troubles be banished
May you help in my quest.
Thank you, so mote it be.

Allow the candle to burn down safely. Leave the figure of your friend on the bay leaf and place this on a windowsill that catches the morning sun. Your friend's troubles should soon diminish.

Please bear in mind that this spell is not a substitute for medical advice. If you feel that your friend needs to speak to a professional, tell her and go along with her.

KNOW YOUR ENEMY

If you've been having a run of bad luck, it could
be that someone is inflicting it on you. It is
important that you know who your enemy is –
don't just guess, as this could send the spell out
to the wrong person and then it will come back
to you. This spell will not harm anyone; it will
simply return any bad vibes that an enemy is
sending out.

YOU WILL NEED:

A handful of salt

A mirror with a stand

One black candle

Matches or a lighter

WHAT YOU DO:

Do this spell on a Saturday or a waning moon.
First and foremost, you need to protect yourself.
To do this, simply cast a circle of salt around
you and ask the Goddess to protect you while
you perform this spell. Place the mirror behind
the black candle, then light the candle. Stare
into the flame and chant the following words
three times:

> *By the count of three*
> *I send this back to thee.*
> *Return to your source*
> *And never return.*
> *One, Two, Three.*

Clap your hands three times above the candle,
and then allow it to burn away – don't move the
mirror until it has done so. This will return
the bad luck sent to you to its original source.

JUST GOOD FRIENDS

If a friend just won't take the hint that you aren't romantically interested in them, try this spell to make them see that you want to be just good friends and nothing more.

YOU WILL NEED:

Something personal to them (such as a photograph, a gift, an item of jewellery or clothing)

Something personal to you

One white tealight

Matches or a lighter

One jasmine incense stick

WHAT YOU DO:

Do this spell on a waning moon. Place the personal items in front of the white tealight. Light it, and then light the incense stick using the flame of the tealight. Wave the incense stick over both lots of personal items and say the following:

I know that you love me
And I love you too
But not in the way
you want me to.
Let us not spoil
what we have now
And remain just good friends
for evermore.

Allow the candle to burn down, then return the personal items to their rightful places. You should soon notice that your friend realises you are not romantically interested in them, but will always be there for them.

GOSSIP, GOSSIP, GO AWAY

We all love hearing juicy gossip about other
people, but if that chat turns out to be malicious,
it can be hurtful and destructive to the victim.
If someone is throwing shade at you by spreading
rumours, try this simple spell to banish the
gossip and protect you from the perpetrator.

YOU WILL NEED:

A slip of paper with
the gossip's name on it

A mixing dish

One red pepper

One green pepper

One strong onion

A knife

A teaspoon of pepper

A freezer or ice box

WHAT YOU DO:

Do this spell on a Saturday. Place the slip
of paper in the dish, then chop up the peppers
and onion all over it. Next, add the teaspoon of
pepper and stir the mixture around. The pepper
is a banishing ingredient and the onion acts
as a protective ingredient.

As you mix, say the following words:

May your tongue be sour from your gossip
May your words return to you
May you realize the pain you have caused
And harm no one again.

Place the dish and its contents in the freezer
or ice box for 24 hours, then discard the
mixture in the waste bin.

LOVING YOURSELF
CHARM

How can we expect to have a happy relationship
when we don't love ourselves? Everybody has
hang-ups, but you shouldn't let them damage
your sense of self-worth. This is a confidence-
booster spell for those times when we feel
unhappy with something about ourselves.

YOU WILL NEED:

A bunch of brightly
coloured flowers

Five white tealight
candles

A tall mirror

WHAT YOU DO:

Find a time when you can do this spell
undisturbed. Arrange the flowers in a circle on
the floor – big enough for you to sit in. Arrange
the tealight candles in a smaller circle within
the flower circle.

Place the mirror outside of the circle in
such a way that you can see yourself when you
are inside the circle. Sit cross-legged within
the circle and carefully light all five candles.
Look at yourself in the mirror and see how
beautiful you really are. See your inner beauty.
Repeat the following chant five times:

I am beautiful,
no matter what anyone says.
I am filled with love for myself
in every single way.

Close your eyes and imagine yourself surrounded by a warm orange glow. Allow the warm glow to absorb into your body. Feel how warm and wonderful you now feel inside. This is your inner beauty being restored. Allow yourself to simply be here as long as you like.

Did you know?

The circle is an important symbol in witchcraft. Witches often create a 'magick circle' at gatherings where they practise their rituals, celebrate calendar festivals and enhance their magickal powers. To protect themselves when practising magick, witches may also cast a protective circle around themselves using salt water and candles.

FAKE IT AND MAKE IT SPELL

Very few people are lucky enough to be born with
the natural confidence that allows them to go
into new situations without any fear. The rest
of us just have to fake it and do our best, while
fighting the self-doubt that causes this anxiety.
This is the simplest of spells, and it helps you to
tackle the things that are holding you back from
being your best self.

YOU WILL NEED:

Somewhere quiet where
you can relax for
half an hour

WHAT YOU DO:

You can do this spell any time and anywhere.
Close your eyes and imagine there's a big white
cinema screen in front of you. On the screen,
place images of any negative thoughts you
have about yourself – this could be something
physical, like thinking you're not pretty
enough, or to do with your abilities, like
thinking you're not clever or funny enough.

Now imagine that you have a big red marker
pen in your hand. Scribble each negative image
out with the pen, so that you can no longer see
them. Now the cinema screen is completely white
again and you are going to place only positive
images on it. Put anything and everything
that you desire to be true on this new screen.

If you wish you were taller or shorter, fatter or thinner, were more graceful or had a less foghorn-like sneeze, then place the image of the 'best you' on your screen. Forget that it's not 'true' – this will be the way you portray yourself to others in the future. If you do this ritual for two weeks, you will notice that your confidence and self-worth will soar – and others will notice it, too.

Did you know?

Many witches have an altar in their home as a place to do their spellwork, or to keep symbols of their power, elemental treasures from places special to them or crystals that connect to a particular healing practice.

THE WITCH'S CALENDAR

Wiccans connect with the earth and the seasons through what is known as the 'Wheel of the Year' (represented by the symbol of an eight-spoked wheel), which is a cycle of eight festival days (sabbats) that divide the year and mark the changing of the season and the lunar calendar. During a sabbat festival, a gathering will mark the season change or mid-season point with appropriate celebration of the gods and goddesses and Mother Nature.

THE FOUR GREATER SABBATS

Samhain: The Druids' New Year, marked at sundown on October 31st, and celebrated in many cultures as Halloween, All Hallow's Eve, All Soul's Day or *Dia de los Muertos* (Day of the Dead). The Wiccan festival marks the rising of Samhain (the Lord of Darkness) from the underworld and notes the thin line between the living world and the spiritual realm. As marking the opening of the 'dark' half of the year, it is the time when loved ones who have passed over are remembered and celebrated.

Imbolc: Commemorating Brigid, the Celtic goddess of fire and fertility, this festival on February 2nd notes the increasing strength of the sun, and allies with the festivals of Candlemas and Groundhog Day in the US.

Beltane: Originally celebrated on May 5th but now coinciding with May Day, Beltane celebrates the god and goddess of fertility as summer approaches.

Lammas: Sometimes known as Lughnasadh or August Eve and celebrated on August 1st, this festival celebrates the first harvest of the season. From 'loaf-day', Wiccans celebrate the first wheat harvest and the gifts of the god and goddess.

THE FOUR LESSER SABBATS

Yule: The Winter Solstice (December 21st), and the shortest day of the year. Wiccan celebrations include mistletoe, yule logs, yule trees and lots of candles.

Eostara: The Spring Equinox (March 21st) is when the hours of daylight are equal to the hours of darkness.

Litha: The Summer Solstice (June 21st) marks the highest point of the sun and the longest day.

Mabon: The Autumn Equinox (September 21st) notes the Harvest Festival and celebrates the birth of Mabon, the son of Mordon the Goddess of Earth, at the Feast of Mabon.

In the Southern Hemisphere, Witches celebrate the opposite holidays as their seasons change. As the Northern Hemisphere marks the Spring Equinox, the Southern Hemisphere notes the Fall/Autumn Equinox, and so on.

You will learn to work with the seasons and use their passing in your magick. Witches often cast rituals and spells with the cycles of the earth or the phases of the moon to intenisfy their intent and power.

BANISH A BULLY

If you find that you're the victim of a bully,
whether at school or work, then this spell
will work a treat. You cannot hurt anyone
with white magick, but this powerful spell
will make the person who has been bullying
you think twice about doing it again.

YOU WILL NEED:

A permanent black
marker pen

A piece of white paper

A matchbox

A bag of salt

One black candle

A candle holder

Matches or a lighter

A small mirror

A 15 cm (6") length
of black ribbon

WHAT YOU DO:

Do this spell on a waning or a new moon. First of
all, take your black marker pen and write on the
paper in big letters the name of the person who
is bullying you. Next, colour in the matchbox
in black marker pen. Sit on the floor and cast a
big circle of salt around you. Place the black
candle (in a holder), your piece of paper, the
matchbox, the mirror and the black ribbon in
the circle with you. Light the candle and rip
the piece of paper up into tiny pieces. When
you've done this, put all the pieces of paper in
the matchbox. Take a pinch of salt from your
circle and put this in the matchbox too. Now tie
the matchbox up with the black ribbon. Place
the matchbox on top of the mirror and say the
following words:

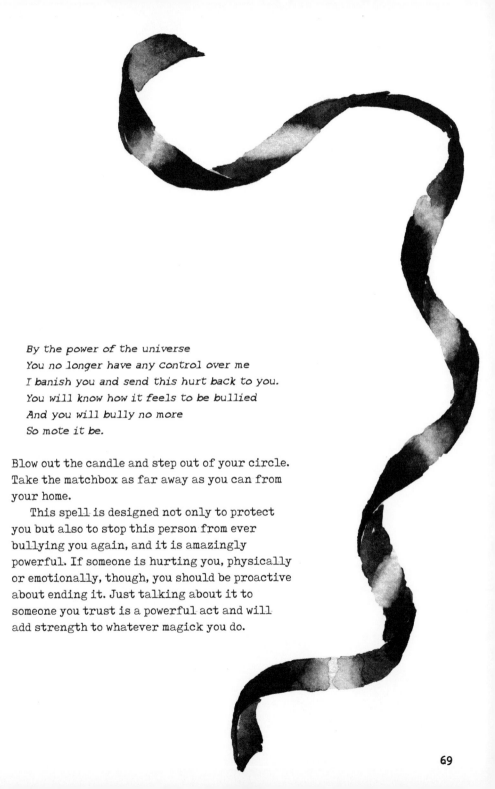

By the power of the universe
You no longer have any control over me
I banish you and send this hurt back to you.
You will know how it feels to be bullied
And you will bully no more
So mote it be.

Blow out the candle and step out of your circle.
Take the matchbox as far away as you can from
your home.

    This spell is designed not only to protect
you but also to stop this person from ever
bullying you again, and it is amazingly
powerful. If someone is hurting you, physically
or emotionally, though, you should be proactive
about ending it. Just talking about it to
someone you trust is a powerful act and will
add strength to whatever magick you do.

POWER OF PERSUASION

It's possible to influence someone without their knowing about it, and this spell is designed to do just that. Use this spell wisely, though – don't try to influence everyone you come across, because magick shouldn't be seen as the easy solution to everything.

YOU WILL NEED:

One sheet of gold or yellow paper

Scissors

A pen

Nine gold tealights

Matches or a lighter

WHAT YOU DO:

Start this nine-day spell on a Sunday. Cut the sheet of gold or yellow paper lengthways, about 5 cm (2"), so that you have a long strip of paper. On this write the name of the person you wish to influence and what you wish the outcome of your quest to be. Place the nine gold tealights on top of the strip of paper on a windowsill, or somewhere else they won't be moved, because this spell needs to be left undisturbed for the full duration. On the Sunday that you start the spell, light the first tealight and say the following words nine times:

[Name of person],
You shall grant my desire
You shall grant my wish
Your power cannot resist.
By the power of this fire
you shall grant my desire.
So mote it be.

Allow the tealight to burn down and then leave it. On the following eight nights perform the same ritual until all the tealights have burned down. Your wish will soon be granted.

GETTING SOME SPACE

Some people just can't take 'No' for an answer, can they? This spell is designed to stop someone pestering you, when a subtle hint doesn't work.

YOU WILL NEED:

One teaspoon of sea salt

One dark blue candle

Matches or a lighter

Two drops of lavender oil

A hair from the person who is bothering you (or a sample of handwriting)

A heatproof dish

WHAT YOU DO:

Do this spell on a waning moon, and on a Saturday if possible.

You can obtain a hair from the person in question from his or her hairbrush or from their clothes – failing that, try to get a sample of their signature or at least a piece of handwriting. Cast a circle of salt round the blue candle – this will protect you. Light the candle, then rub the lavender oil onto the palms of your hands – this will also protect you from any negative reactions.

Take the sample of hair or handwriting and set it alight in the flame from the candle. Allow it to burn completely by dropping it into the heatproof dish. Say the following three times:

[Name of person] be gone from my life
It is now time to move on
And let me do the same.
You will be out of my life from this day forth
And never bother me again.

Allow the candle to burn right down and throw
any remaining wax right away from your home. You
should only do this spell if you really don't want
the other person ever to bother you again.

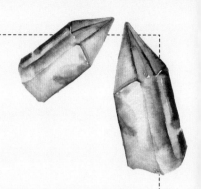

GEMSTONE MAGICK

Do you often wear precious stones? Are you drawn to them, do you collect them or are you often given them by those who know and love you? We are instinctively attracted to stones and gems from an early age, formed by our earth and blessed with notable powers.

From ancient times, wise women and men have used gems as protective talismans, symbols of power and as part of ritual magick, studying them for their properties and healing potential, and giving them complex associations.

Early writings that list gems associated with fertility and birth rituals have been found in ancient civilisations, and all cultures have their own myths around precious stones. Ancient Egyptians often wore gems as jewellery or buried them with their dead. The headdresses of Pharoahs would be lined with green malachite, as it was believed to encourage wisdom and enhance the power of the mind, and the deep blue lapis lazuli was a popular choice for symbolic jewellery and totems as it represented truth, spiritual development, love and peace.

Eastern Asian legends describe dragons with wish-granting pearls, while King Solomon was said to hold an emerald that granted him power over the entire world.

In modern witchcraft, popular choices of gemstones are:

Amethyst, known as the 'All-Purpose Stone', can be worn or placed in your home to instil calm and inspire positive thoughts and dreams.

Citrine is a bright yellow crystal that attracts happiness and warmth; it helps communication between people when placed in the home or workplace.

Jasper grounds the wearer, restores balance and is often used in work-based spells as it represents responsibility and organisation.

Hematite stones are magnetic and so are used in attraction magick.

Moonstones are a milky colour and associated with the power of the moon, intuition, clairvoyance and empathy.

Peridot is a green stone that attracts growth, prosperity and success.

Quartz (clear) is often known as 'The Master Healer' and used to promote cleansing, healing and energy.

Tourmaline is used to clear the aura, stop negative patterns and protect the wearer from harm.

The stones can be worn as magick charms, placed in key areas in the home or workplace, or used to enhance the energy of a spell or ritual. As with most magickal tools, allow yourself to choose the stone that best channels your own energies and intent.

3.

WORK SPELLS

Magick is all about empowerment and fulfilment, so it makes sense to ensure that you are unleashing your powers and creative energies to reach your full potential in the world of work. Whether you are setting up your own company, looking to step into a new career or simply trying to win a promotion, here are some super spells to help you find your way forwards.

While you're casting your spells, remember to listen to messages from the world around you – your career dreams will only come true if they're truly what you want, not if they're what you feel is expected of you or what you should be doing with your life. Remember that magick will only provide what you truly need – there is no spell in the world that's going to land you a six-figure job by the end of the week.

GET THAT
JOB SPELL

Do you spend your wage before it even arrives in your bank? Are you sick of working to death on a job that pays peanuts? Or are you just fed up with being broke all the time and in need of a regular injection of cash? This spell will help you to land a job to suit your needs – whether it's to pay for your everyday living expenses or go on that holiday you've been dreaming of.

YOU WILL NEED:

A piece of green paper

A gold pen

Three mint leaves

A teaspoon of dried sage

One gold or silver candle

A candle holder

Matches or a lighter

WHAT YOU DO:

You should cast this spell on a full moon, waxing moon or on a Thursday. Draw a large pentagram in the centre of your piece of paper with your gold pen – a pentagram is a circle with a five-pointed star inside it. In the centre of the pentagram write the word JOB, making sure the star is pointing upwards not downwards. Around this word write what kind of job you want – part-time, full-time, in an office or outdoors, how many hours, how much you'd like to be paid, and so on. Tear up the mint leaves and put these and the dried sage into the pentagram. Place the candle in a holder on top of the herbs and light it.

Say the following words:

Goddess Morrigan, hear my plea
Send me a job to help my needs
Give me a job that I will love
I send this message to you above.

Allow the candle to burn down. Carefully take the paper with the herbs on it to the nearest window, open the window and blow the contents from the paper into the air.

You will soon hear about or see an advertisement for the ideal job for you.

Did you know?

Christians once used the pentagram as a religious symbol. Each point represented the five wounds of Christ. To pagans and witches it represents Morrigan, the war goddess who fights for peace and good fortune for others. If you see the pentagram drawn with the top point of the star pointing to the bottom of the circle, this represents dark and sinister magick, so always draw your pentagram with the top point of the star pointing upwards.

INTERVIEW
MAGICK

This is a tried-and-tested spell that I have suggested many times for interview success – all the people who have tried it have either secured the job they have been going for or been promoted. It is therefore also suitable if you are going for promotion at your current place of work.

YOU WILL NEED:

A matchbox

A pinch of chopped mint

A pinch of chopped rosemary

A pinch of mixed spice

A pinch of cinnamon

One small silver coin

Some salt water (two teaspoons of salt to 50ml (2fl oz) of water)

One small piece of blue gift wrap

A piece of blue ribbon

One blue candle

Matches or a lighter

WHAT YOU DO:

Prepare this spell the night before your interview. Open the matchbox and place all the herbs and spices inside it. Wash the silver coin in the salted water to cleanse any negativity from it, then place it in the matchbox. Next, wrap up the matchbox in the gift wrap so that it looks like a mini parcel. Tie the blue ribbon round it and secure it. Light the blue candle and say the following three times:

My door to the future is open wide
Your light will guide the way for me
And show me the path to a better future
Where more money and fulfilment await me.

Allow the blue candle to burn down. Before you go to bed, shake the matchbox three times and then sleep with it under your pillow. Prior to your interview the following morning, shake the box again three times. Blue is the colour of luck in the workplace, so for an extra boost, wear something blue on the day. It could be a piece of clothing or just an accessory.

You should sail through with flying colours. However, if you don't get the job, don't panic – it doesn't mean the spell hasn't worked; it simply means this particular job is not for you and that a better one is nearby.

BEWITCH YOUR BUSINESS

This spell is designed to increase the luck of your business, career, or any endeavour you're making money from (or hoping to).

YOU WILL NEED:

One sheet of white card

A pen

Four silver stars (available from most stationers)

Glue

One silver coin

WHAT YOU DO:

Do this spell on a Thursday evening or a waxing moon. The first thing you need to do is write down all the things you want for your business. More clients? More money? More time off? To open your own shop? To work from home?

Think in the future tense and visualise how you want your business to be within the next couple of years. Whatever you want, write it down on the piece of card. Stick one silver star in each corner of the card. Then stick the silver coin on the reverse of the card. Close your eyes and say the following:

> *This manifesto represents the wishes for
>   my business*
> *May you, Lord and Lady, grant me my wishes*
> *May you manifest my dreams*
> *And make the written word reality.*
> *So mote it be.*

Keep your piece of card in a safe place wherever you work – for example, in your desk or with your work equipment. You will now attract opportunities that will in turn grant your wishes. Soon you will be ticking off the desires listed on your business luck card.

Did you know?

Not only is a silver coin representative of fortune, but it conducts energy too, making it an excellent choice to amplify the power of your spells.

YOUR CAREER CANDLE SPELL

If you would like a change of luck in your career, use this spell which is designed to increase the number of opportunities you have to get ahead in your profession.

YOU WILL NEED:

Three bay leaves

A pebble

A gold pen

One gold candle

Matches or a lighter

WHAT YOU DO:

You should do this spell on a Sunday or a full moon. Arrange the three bay leaves to form a triangle shape. Write the word 'luck' on the pebble with the gold pen and place it in the centre of the triangle. Put the gold candle behind the arrangement and light it. Say the following three times:

By this golden light
Make my career bright
Send me golden opportunities
To lighten my life.

Allow the candle to burn down. Throw the bay leaves and any remaining wax away. Place the pebble in your purse, wallet or handbag. Whenever you remember, rub the pebble for increased luck.

LUCKY TRAVEL CHARM

If you travel a lot, this is the perfect charm to take with you to ensure that you have a safe and lucky trip – a traveller should never be without it.

YOU WILL NEED:

Four sticks about 7.5 cm (3") in length

Two sprigs of lavender

One metre (one yard) of green ribbon

Three drops of lavender oil

WHAT YOU DO:

Make this charm on a Thursday. Arrange the four sticks in the shape of a compass. Lay the two sprigs of lavender on top of two of the sticks that cross at the centre of the compass. Then take the piece of green ribbon and tie the sticks and the lavender together, so that it really looks like a compass. Anoint the compass with the lavender oil, and say the following:

Archangel Raphael
Bless this charm with your protection
And protect me when I journey
From north to south and east to west
Guide me so that I travel and return safely.

Whenever you have to travel, take your lucky charm with you. When driving in your car, keep a spare length of ribbon and hang the charm somewhere it will not distract you. When the fragrance of lavender disappears, re-anoint the compass and repeat the words of the spell.

THE TAKE-BACK
SPELL

None of us can predict for certain what will happen when we make a decision, and sometimes – if bad luck is hiding just around the corner – we can regret our actions. This spell is designed for those times when you've done something on the spur of the moment and now wish that you hadn't. This might be something like deciding to chuck in your job or throw your partner out. This candle spell will make everything better again.

Six white candles

Matches or a lighter

Start this spell on a Monday and repeat it over the next five days. Try to do this spell at the same time every day for the six days. Find a time and place where you will not be disturbed. Light the first candle and say the following words:

> *I was foolish*
> *Now I am sane*
> *Banish my decision*
> *And restore things again.*
> *A second chance is what I need*
> *Lord and Lady, help me, please.*

Repeat the ritual on the next five days. After six days something will happen that will make things go back to normal – for example, you will be reinstated in your job (or offered another one), or your partner will call you and you'll make up. That being said, I always believe that things happen to us for a reason, so although you may have regretted what you've said or done, it might have been the right time for a change.

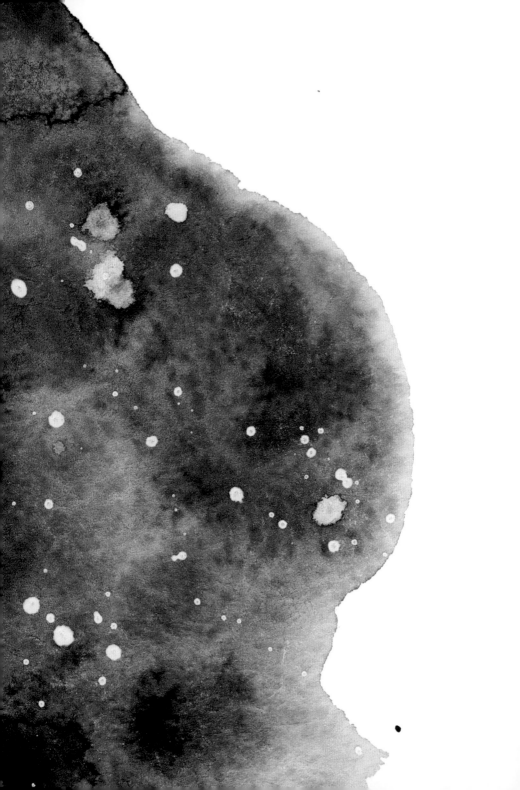

NEW JOB WISH

Being unemployed can be one of the most stressful situations you ever face, and it can make you feel depressed and disillusioned with life. If you have been unemployed for a while, do this spell to turn your luck around.

YOU WILL NEED:

One dark blue candle

- -

Your unemployment card or letter

- -

A crystal

- -

Matches or a lighter

- -

One freezer bag

- -

A freezer or ice box

- -

WHAT YOU DO:

Do this spell on a new moon. Place the items in the following order: the blue candle at the back; your unemployment card or letter in front of the candle; and the crystal on top of the card. Light the blue candle and stare into the crystal. Send all your worries about being unemployed into the crystal – let it absorb everything you feel negative about. When you feel ready, say the following words once:

This is just a phase in my life
It will pass as quickly as it came.
I no longer feel disillusioned about this situation
This crystal absorbs all my bad luck.

Allow the candle to burn down. Finally, place your unemployment card or letter in the freezer bag, then secure the bag and leave it overnight in the freezer or ice box. You should soon see an improvement in your employment prospects.

A LUCKY AUDITION

Everyone needs a little luck in their lives,
but you'll be especially aware of it if you are
attending auditions. You might be an aspiring
actor, a musician or a vocalist. Whichever is
the case, try this spell for success at your next
audition – just remember me when you're flying
high in Hollywood.

YOU WILL NEED:

A piece of gold card

Scissors

A pen

Silver sequins

Glue

One gold candle

One silver candle

One metre (one yard)
of thin gold ribbon

Matches or a lighter

WHAT YOU DO:

Do this spell on a Sunday night or a full moon.
Cut a large star shape out of the piece of gold
card and, in the centre of it, write your name.
Stick silver sequins all round the edge of the
star so that it glitters. Place your star on a
windowsill or a table, then put the gold candle
to the left of the star and the silver candle to
the right. Place the thin gold ribbon in front
of the star.

Light both candles and say the following:

Star light, star bright
Grant my wish for me tonight.
Stardom beckons just for me
Grant this wish, so mote it be.

Allow both candles to burn down. Stick the gold
star to the door of your bedroom and imagine
this as your dressing room door. Visualise how
life will be when you become a success – your
luxury trailer and personal assistant, signing
autographs, bowing to your audience, and so on.

The spell is now complete. The only thing you
need to remember, when you go for an audition,
is to take the piece of gold ribbon along with
you. While you are waiting, hold the ribbon in
your hands and tie 13 random knots in it. If you
have to wait a long time, undo the knots one by
one and tie them again. Keep visualising your
success in the audition and life as a star.

EXAM EXCELLENCE

This is an ideal spell to perform if you, or someone you know, has an exam coming up. It will work on anything from a driving test to the final exams of a degree course.

YOU WILL NEED:

One gold candle

One cinnamon incense stick

Matches or a lighter

A small purse or pouch

WHAT YOU DO:

Do this spell on a Wednesday. Find a time and a quiet place where you will not be disturbed for half an hour. Light the gold candle and the incense stick and close your eyes. Imagine yourself sitting in the room where you are to take your exam or test. Concentrate on your breathing and listen as you breathe in and out. When you inhale, try to breathe from your stomach rather than your chest.

Imagine yourself being completely relaxed and able to pass this exam or test with ease. Imagine you have done the test many times and can easily pass it. When you are satisfied that you have visualised enough, allow the candle to burn down until there is 2.5 cm (1") of wax left. Place the remaining wax in your purse or pouch. You need to take this with you when you go for your test or exam.

Just before your exam, allow ten minutes to visualise the same images you created when you started the spell. Tell yourself that you have passed your test and that you are just going through the necessary steps to gain that certificate or licence. Make sure you concentrate on your breathing and, above all, stay relaxed.

LOSING YOUR JOB SPELL

Even though we are persistently made aware of the lack of security in the modern workplace, it can still be a shock to discover that you have been laid off. It's not the end of the world, though. Banish the bad luck that has caused you to lose your job by performing this simple spell, then perform a spell to change your luck from bad to good.

YOU WILL NEED:

Your old employment contract

A red pen

A pinch of black pepper

One black candle

Matches or a lighter

WHAT YOU DO:

Do this spell on a waning moon. Find a time when you can be alone with your thoughts for ten minutes. Open up your old contract and draw red lines right through every page. Then sprinkle a pinch of black pepper over it, and fold it up four times. Light the black candle, and say the following words six times:

My bad luck will leave
I banish you to the depths
This is now in the past
And I am ready to start afresh.

Wait until the candle has burned right down and, just before it extinguishes itself, pour a few drops of hot wax onto the contract to seal it. The following day bury it somewhere away from your home.

EMERGENCY FUNDS

We all have times in our lives when we have more
money going out than coming in. This is a spell
designed for general use when you discover that you
are having bad luck financially. It could be that
you simply don't have enough money to see you through
to your next pay day, or that you are facing the
prospect of bankruptcy.

Do this spell to banish financial bad luck, then try
the spell for financial luck from page 82.

YOU WILL NEED:

A photocopy of a
recent bank statement

- -

A black pen

- -

A photocopy of a
recent bill

- -

Glue

- -

A handful of red
glitter

- -

One dark blue candle

- -

Continued >

WHAT YOU DO:

Do this spell on a new moon. Take the photocopy
of your recent bank statement and cross out
any amounts that show you are in debt, changing
them to a credit with a black pen. Next, take the
photocopy of a recent bill and write across it
in big black letters the word 'paid'. Place these
two photocopies on a table and paste some glue
all over them.

Next, sprinkle red glitter over both copies.
Put the blue candle on top of the copies and
light it. Say the following words:

By the time this spell is done
My finances will improve.
I banish all debt to the universe
May you help in my quest to
Remove these financial obstacles
from my life.

Matches or a lighter

A photocopy of your
bank card

A handful of silver
glitter

Allow the candle to burn down. Next, put
the photocopy of your bank card on top of the
copies of your bank statement and bill. Paste a
small amount of glue on top of the copy of your
card then sprinkle the silver glitter on top and
say the following words:

By the power of this spell
I banish poverty from my life
Leaving only room for prosperity
  to flourish.
This is my quest, so mote it be.

Leave the pile undisturbed for 24 hours
to enable the message to be carried to the
universe. Tidy your spell away and keep the
photocopied documents and glitter together in
your financial folder. You should notice an
improvement in your finances within 29 days.

A WITCH'S GARDEN

We talk a lot about witchcraft being a nature-based religion and its origins as a healing force. While twenty-first-century witchcraft is something different, we still want to embrace nature and use it to heal and restore. We may no longer wake with the sun and eat with the seasons, but using nature in our spellcasting aids our natural connection with the universe's energies and helps ground us.

A GARDEN SPACE

Create a garden space – even if it's just a windowsill – where you can grow some magickal herbs and plants and bring nature into your life. If you have room, why not add a natural altar or sanctuary – a garden seat, tree stump or green candle is sufficient to give your green space a spiritual centre.

Witches would once have had a huge apothecary of herbs, spices, botanicals and other natural forms in their gardens and storerooms in the past, but you don't need to worry about using special ingredients today. Did you know that Shakespeare's witches' famous incantation 'Eye of newt and toe of frog' actually refers to mustard seeds and a type of buttercup plant – nothing you couldn't track down.

HERBS

Every herb and root has medicinal properties or magickal associations, so research what would help you most. Many herbs at the supermarket or grown your own on a sunny windowsill (south-facing is ideal). Magickal favourites are:

Sage: A wonderful herb for cleansing and banishing bad energy. Hang a bunch in your home near the entry point, or sprinkle handfuls of sage and salt in a clockwise direction around the outside of your home.

Basil: Often used in money and prosperity spells and to aid happiness at home. You can add it to a bath or soak it in water for two days then wash your doorstep with the water.

Lavender: Used to calm and purify. Try hanging it above your bed or using lavender water in your spells.

Rosemary: A powerful protection herb and supporter of women. Plant it in your garden for fidelity and strong relationships, and use it in cooking, purification baths and rituals.

TREES

There are long-standing connections between witchcraft and trees. Witches' wands are often made from hazel as it represents spiritual connection; the willow tree is known as the healing tree and an apple tree in your garden will bless your home.

The oak tree has long been associated with ancient magick, as the wood of King Arthur's round table and the meeting place for druids. Its leaves, branches and acorns represent the gods and it has notable healing properties. Elm brings stability and grounding to a spell, while the Nordic World Tree (Yggdrasil) is an ash tree.

Tend to your garden and harvest your herbs under the light of the full moon to get the most energy from your gifts from nature.

4.

HOME AND FAMILY SPELLS

If you're just entering the world of magick, using it to protect your home and those you love most is a great way to start your spell casting, and one of the most worthwhile uses of your new power. Here are some spells to help you secure your dream home, look after all who live there and bring luck to your most precious sanctuary. Whether you're worried about storm damage or difficult neighbours, using earth and air magick will restore your space and bring harmony.

YOUR LUCKY HOME

Some homes are said to be unlucky, but no one needs to live in a place where bad luck comes and goes all the time. This spell will encourage luck to come into your home. After doing it, you should notice a difference in the atmosphere.

YOU WILL NEED:

Five sprigs of rosemary

Five sprigs of parsley

Five sprigs of lavender

One metre (one yard) of green ribbon

WHAT YOU DO:

Do this spell on a Monday or a waning moon, if possible. If you've bought or picked them fresh, dry the herbs by placing them in a warm oven (110°C/225°F) or an airing cupboard. When they are dry, gather them all together and tie them in a bunch using the green ribbon. Don't cut off any of the ribbon – leave it trailing from the bunch of herbs, as this will encourage good luck into your home. Place the bunch of herbs above your doorway, and say the following:

Only good luck may pass through this house
Bad luck is not permitted.
My Lord and Lady, encourage the flow of
    good luck
To our home.

When your lucky herbs are looking a bit tired, repeat the spell with a fresh sprig.

FINDING A PERFECT HOME

This spell will help you find the home that
is most suited to you, and will also help with
finances so that you are able to buy or rent it.

YOU WILL NEED:

Three orange candles

One small toy house
(available from most
toy stores)

Three mint leaves

Three sprigs of
lavender

Matches or a lighter

WHAT YOU DO:

Do this spell on a Friday, a Monday or a waxing
moon. Arrange the three candles round the toy
house. Place the mint leaves and the sprigs of
lavender close to the house. Light the three
candles, moving in a clockwise direction. As the
flames rise, visualise your dream home being
available to you. It doesn't matter if you don't
have the necessary funds right now – try not
to think about that. Imagine that you have the
power to create the finances you need to buy
the property you want.

Visualise phoning the removal men to pack
up your old home, and arriving at your new
dream home. Imagine putting the key in the
front door of your new house, walking in and
feeling instantly at home.

When you feel you can visualise no more,
leave the room and allow the candles to burn
safely down. Keep your toy house, mint and
lavender wherever you keep your house keys.
You will soon notice something happening that
will enable you to buy your new home.

MOVING ON SPELL

In the ever-changing housing market you can always do with a bit of luck in selling your home. This little ritual will help the sale of your property to run smoothly.

YOU WILL NEED:

One crystal

Some salt water (two teaspoons of salt to 50ml (2fl oz) of water)

A photograph of the front of your property

One white candle

Matches or a lighter

WHAT YOU DO:

Do this spell for six days, starting on a Monday or a full moon. First, you need to cleanse your crystal by soaking it in the salt water. Leave the crystal in the solution while you prepare the rest of the spell.

Place the photograph of your house under the white candle, then light the candle. Say the following three times:

My home is available to you now
I no longer need it
Come and see.
This happy home is calling to you
May you desire it to be your home.
So mote it be.

Blow the candle out and reuse it over the next five days, repeating the incantation each time. Then dry the crystal and place it in a prominent part of your house.

When prospective buyers come to view your house, the crystal will emit this positive energy to them.

HOME PROTECTION
SPELL

Even though it might be new to you, your home might still have negative vibes floating around from a previous occupant. This cleansing and protection spell will cleanse any negativity from your home and protect it from intruders, fire, floods or any other unwanted intrusions.

YOU WILL NEED:

100g (3½oz) of salt

500ml (16fl oz) of bottled water

A jug

A whole onion

A knife

One seashell for every room

WHAT YOU DO:

Cast this spell on a new moon or a Saturday. Pour the salt into the water and shake gently. Next, pour the salted water into a jug. Now cut the onion into four quarters. Sprinkle a few drops of salted water onto each quarter of onion and place one quarter in each corner of the main room you use in your apartment. Sprinkle each seashell with the salt mixture and place a seashell in every room in your home.

Finally, walk into each room and sprinkle a few drops of the salted water into each room.

Say the following words as you enter each room:

This room is now protected and cleansed.

Leave the onion in the main room for one week as this will absorb any negativity in the home. Leave the seashells where they are and every so often re-cleanse them with a new protection salt mixture. Your home will now be magickally insured and protected.

Did you know?

Decluttering your home is good for you in many magickal ways. Stale and negative energies get stuck in cluttered corners or linger after difficult guests visit your home. Having a good clear up, placing crystals such as clear quartz in dark corners and using sage to cleanse the air will make your home happier and your mind much clearer.

TO REMOVE
A HAUNTING

Are you feeling unsettled in your home, or as if someone else is there with you? Occasionally a past life can be so unsettled that a spirit will try to upset someone in this world. Known as 'lost souls', such spirits haven't yet managed – or are reluctant – to find their way into the spirit world; they are often disturbed or don't realise they have passed on. If you have been experiencing a run of bad luck and can't pinpoint anyone in the living world who might wish to harm you, try this spell to banish a spirit to his or her rightful home.

Silver foil

Scissors

A ballpoint pen

One silver candle

Some salt water (two
teaspoons of salt to
50ml (2fl oz) of water)

A handful of salt

Matches or a lighter

Do this spell on a waning moon. Cut a large circle, big enough to place your candle on, out of the silver foil. Write the words 'Go Home' with the ballpoint pen on the foil, then turn it over (this is to reflect the bad luck back where it came from). Place the silver candle on top of the silver foil.

Before you light the candle, take the salt water and sprinkle every room in your house with a few drops. Sit in front of the candle and cast a big circle of salt round you – make sure the circle is not broken while you do this spell.

Now light your candle and say the following:

I realise it is not your fault
But it is time for you to move on now.
Please go through the light
To your new resting place
Never to return again.
Happy journey

Give yourself five minutes to remain in the protection circle and then you can move out of it. Allow the candle to burn down.

Your bad luck should be banished within 24 hours. If you you remain feeling uneasy, repeat the spell.

PET PROTECTION
SPELL

Cats are said to be lucky enough to have nine lives, but what about all the other living creatures we adopt as our pets? This spell will ensure that your cat, dog, hamster or even your goldfish enjoys a healthy, happy life.

YOU WILL NEED:

One rose-scented candle

One feather

One rose incense stick and holder (or secure the stick with a small piece of removable adhesive)

Something to represent your pet (a collar, feeding bowl, photograph)

Matches or a lighter

WHAT YOU DO:

Do this spell on a Tuesday or a new moon. This is an outdoor spell, so you need to do it on a day when it's not going to rain, or the water will extinguish the candle.

Find a nice quiet spot in the garden and arrange the objects as follows: place the candle in the centre; put the feather behind the candle; place the incense stick and holder in front of the candle; put the item that represents your pet in front of the incense stick. Light the candle, then the incense stick, and say the following words:

Did you know?

The rabbit's foot was always considered
to be a powerful and lucky charm and
a protector against evil. Rabbits are
born with their eyes wide open, and it was
believed that this meant they could see
evil approaching, before anything else
could see it.

Goddess, Creator of nature
May you hear my call.
Protect [name of pet] and all living
  creatures
No harm may come to all.
So mote it be.

Allow the candle to burn down. Wave the object
that represents your pet through the smoke of
the rose-scented incense and do the same with
the feather.

Your pet should always be lucky and
protected in life from now on.

LOST KEYS SPELL

At best, it can be annoying to realise that you've lost something important; at worst, it can be devastating. I've found missing car keys, lost documents, money and endless other items using this spell.

One red apple

- -

One green apple

- -

A knife

- -

Half a metre (half a yard) green ribbon

- -

One green candle

- -

Matches or a lighter

- -

WHAT YOU DO:

You should do this spell on a Sunday or a full moon.

Cut the red apple in half, then cut the green apple in half. Pair up the opposite colours, so that you have one apple that is half-red and half-green. Tie the apple together with the green ribbon. Light the green candle, and say the following only once:

By the powers of the universe
Come search the land and sea
For what belongs to me.
Show me the path to what I seek
And in return I offer this gift so sweet.

Bury the apple in the garden and eat the other two halves. Now forget all about the lost item – it will turn up when you least expect it.

LUCKY GNOME

Tradition has it that gnomes are mischievous little things. They are magickal little things, too! You can release the magick from the humble gnome by performing this ritual in your garden – you will soon see how much luck your gnome brings you.

YOU WILL NEED:

One garden gnome

- -

100ml (3½fl oz) salt water (four teaspoons of salt to 100ml (3½fl oz) water)

- -

A name for your gnome

- -

WHAT YOU DO:

Do this spell on a full moon. First, cleanse your gnome by washing him in half of the salt water. Next, take your gnome out into the garden and place him or her in a spot where you like to sit. When you have thought of a good name for your gnome (mine is Hamish), gently pour the remaining salt water over him. Before the water dries, repeat the following words three times:

By the magick of three
I give life to thee.
When I pat you three
You will bring luck to me.

You have now released the power of magick in your gnome.

Every time you need a little extra luck in your life, pat your lucky gnome three times and your wish will be granted.

HOME WISHING
PYRAMID

This spell is a modern version of a wishing spell that has been used with great success for many years. The shape of the pyramid is believed by cultures all over the world to have magickal powers and was especially believed by the Egyptians to hold mystical and unexplained powers.

YOU WILL NEED:

A computer with a word processor

WHAT YOU DO:

Cast this spell on any day of the week. Create a new document in your word processor and name it 'My Wish'. Open your document and think of the wish you would like to be granted. Now write the spell in the same way as I have illustrated below, using centred text. For this example I am creating a wish for a happy home:

I wish
I wish for
I wish for a
I wish for a happy
I wish for a happy home

As you can see, from the words I've used to grant my wish I've created a magickal pyramid. Now click the save button to save your wish.

The next time you use your computer, take a moment to go into your document. Underneath the first pyramid leave two clear lines of space and create a second pyramid in the same way. Continue to do this once every day until you end up with several pyramids. The more times you create this repeated wish the more powerful it will become. Keep doing this until your wish is granted.

Did you know?

Modern witchcraft has adapted itself to twenty-first-century life and embraced technology, using social media as a means of bringing witches together and swapping spells. You can also use technology to cast a spell by emailing it to yourself or using any messaging app to send it to the universe.

HAPPY FAMILIES

Nobody wants to fight – really we all love each other and want to get along. Unfortunately, for some the home doesn't feel like a safe and friendly place. Whether you have problems with your parents, a brother or sister, or someone else within your family, try this protection spell to protect you from being hurt, physically or mentally, and create a happy home life for yourself. If you feel that you are in danger or if you are being abused, either physically or mentally, please talk to someone who can help – for example, a teacher, your doctor, the parent of a friend, call a helpline or seek help from someone you trust. Talking to people can make you feel vulnerable, but in fact it makes you stronger.

YOU WILL NEED:

A bag of salt

A bowl

One teaspoon of
cinnamon

One basil leaf

One onion

A knife

One blue candle

One white candle

One green candle

Three candle holders

Matches or a lighter

A 30 cm (12") length
of blue ribbon

WHAT YOU DO:

Do this spell on a waning moon or on a Thursday. And it's best to perform this spell when there is no one else in the house. If this proves difficult, perform it in your bedroom or anywhere you can be private. Pour half of the salt into the bowl and add the cinnamon and the basil leaf. Cut the onion in half and cover both halves of the onion in the salt and cinnamon mixture. Put the three candles into holders, and light them in this order – blue, green then white. Say the following words just once:

Athena, warrior Goddess of order and peace
Hear my cry and take hold of this situation
Banish any negativity from my home
So that I feel safe and secure once again.
May you protect me always
And release positive energy, healing and peace
Let no evil come into my home
So mote it be.

While you wait for the candles to burn down, take the mixture with the salt and cinnamon in it and sprinkle it in every room in the house. Go outside and sprinkle as much of the mixture as you can around the outside of your home.

Take the two onion halves and tie them together with the blue ribbon. Place the onion and the basil leaf under your bed or hide it somewhere in your room.

This powerful spell will banish the fear of going home, protect you from harm and promote harmony in your home life.

FORTUNE TELLING AND DIVINATION

Wouldn't it be great to know what was going to happen to you, or the answer to a question about the future? Well you can learn to read your own future and that of your friends with some simple divination tools.

—

Whether you choose to read tarot cards, a crystal ball or tea leaves, take this opportunity to tune into your hopes and dreams, and to steer your destiny – don't assume that the outcome is set in stone. All forms of divination should be seen as a guide to the possible outcome if you continue on your current path. The most important thing to remember is to follow your own intuition and trust what you feel inside.

These tools will guide you, but they won't automatically make something happen for you or make a decision, only you can do that. Here are a few tools that you may like to try.

THE TAROT

Choose a tarot set that appeals to you, and familiarise yourself before you do any readings. To do a simple question-and-answer spread, think of a question you want answered, then when you feel ready, pick out six cards from anywhere in the pack and lay them face down in front of you. Then pick out one last card which is your outcome card.

Now, starting from the left, turn over the card and read the meanings. In order, they represent: your current situation, what you want, what you fear, what may help you, what may be a disadvantage. These first five cards give you insight into your situation; the final card represents the outcome of your question.

THE PENDULUM

Divination by pendulum is an ancient practice that has been used successfully for years. All you need is a gold or silver ring belonging to you, a 30 cm (12") length of cotton thread and a white tealight candle.

You thread the ring onto the thread and then tie a knot. To find out how the pendulum answers yes and no, ask a simple question such as 'Is the sun hot?' and swing the ring above the candle (being careful not to burn the string). After a few seconds, the ring will either swing from left to right or in a circle. This will tell you how your pendulum tells you 'yes'. Do the same with a simple 'no' question. Then you are ready to ask your pendulum your own questions.

THE TEA LEAVES

It's simple and fun to read tea leaves. All you need is a small teapot, a wide-mouthed cup (not a mug) and saucer, a teabag or tea leaves and boiled water. Just rip open the teabag and pour the loose tea into the teapot, then pour the boiling water over the top. Allow it to brew for a minute while you think about what question you want the reading to answer, then pour the tea. Drink it all except for about a teaspoonful left at the bottom. Now, hold the cup in your left hand and swirl the cup and contents in an anticlockwise circle three times. Turn the cup upside down on the saucer and leave for a minute. Now, lift the cup and 'read' the pattern left. Shapes such as a horseshoe, acorn, bird, crown and flower are good; if you see a bat, owl, rat, dagger or snake, it's not so good.

5.

DESTINY AND FORTUNE SPELLS

We always assume that when good things happen unexpectedly in our lives, it is all down to luck. How many times have you heard people say, 'You lucky thing' or 'That was a stroke of luck'? People who are positive by nature, and who believe in themselves and their dreams, tend to live healthier and fuller lives and appear to get all the lucky breaks by being in the right place at the right time. Conversely, people who appear always to be down on their luck tend to expect bad things to happen to them. In the same way that magick and belief work hand in hand, the kind of luck you have all comes down to the power of the mind.

This section is dedicated to bringing you good luck – whether that is a boost of luck in your health or luck in love. Try out these lucky talismans, charms and rituals to focus your most positive mental energies and increase your luck in every area of your life.

CRYSTAL TALISMAN

A talisman is simply an item that a person believes to be lucky. Talismans have been around for hundreds of years, and whether it's a lucky rabbit's foot or a special coin, if the owner believes it is lucky, then it will be. Crystals hold their own special magickal power, and this talisman is created using a crystal to give it extra magickal luck. Carry this charm with you whenever you need some luck in your life.

YOU WILL NEED:

One crystal (as large as you can find or afford)

50ml (2fl oz) bottled water

Two drops of each of the following oils: rose, lavender and tea tree

----

WHAT YOU DO:

You can do this spell at any time – it's a really easy, but very powerful, spell.

Take the crystal and wash it thoroughly in the bottled water. This completely cleanses it and takes away any negative energy that it may have picked up in the place where you found or bought it. Put two drops of each oil onto the crystal and gently rub them in. When you have done this, hold the crystal in your cupped hands and say six times:

Lucky crystal
By your power bring me your luck.

Keep your crystal in a safe place in your home. When the smell of the oils disappears, you can repeat the spell, remembering to cleanse the crystal first.

ELIXIR OF HEALTH

Good health can't be bought, no matter how much money you have, so it's always handy to have a little spell to keep you in tip-top condition. This one makes a refreshing cup of tea packed with magickal feel-better ingredients. The spell is intended as a helping hand to keep you in good health – but it's not an alternative to going to see the doctor.

YOU WILL NEED:

A cup of boiled water

- -

One green tea teabag

- -

One teaspoon of honey

- -

One mint leaf

- -

One bay leaf

- -

WHAT YOU DO:

Do this whenever you feel unwell, or to encourage good health. Boil a cupful of water and allow it to cool slightly. Place the teabag in the water and leave it to brew for five minutes. Take the teabag out and stir in the teaspoon of honey. Place the mint leaf and bay leaf in the cup and leave for another five minutes. Then hold your hands round the cup and say the following:

Lord and Lady
of the universe
May you bring me
good health.
May you keep illness away
And disease at bay.
Thank you, so mote it be.

Take the mint and bay leaves out and then sip your cup of goodness. Green tea helps to aid digestion, while the honey will give your immune system a boost, the mint leaf will promote a prosperous life and the bay leaf will keep illness at bay.

LUCKY LOTTERY WIN

Don't get too excited – this charm will not guarantee a huge win when gambling. It will, however, increase your chances of winning if you play the lottery or enter any competition. When it comes to the odds, remember that few us actually need a win on the lottery. Yes, we could all do with some extra cash from time to time, but magick works best when there is a genuine need for something in our lives. However, the Goddess likes a little flutter from time to time too, and so long as you don't abuse her powers, she will help you to boost your income with this lucky winning charm.

YOU WILL NEED:

A piece of green card

A green pen

One silver coin

Sticky tape

Clear adhesive
acrylic

WHAT YOU DO:

Do this spell on a Friday night. Ideally you want a lucky four-leafed clover, but as they are pretty hard to find you are going to make one yourself – it may feel like cheating but because it comes directly from you it should actually be helpful.

First of all, draw your four-leafed clover on the piece of card with your green pen. It needs to be small enough to fit in your purse or wallet. Then tape the silver coin to the back of the clover leaf and write around the coin the words 'Lottery Luck' as many times as space will permit. Then cover it with the clear adhesive acrylic to keep the coin clean and protected.

Now, depending on whether you are right- or left-handed, hold the clover in your more dominant hand and close your eyes. Visualise

pushing luck power into the palm of your hand. As you do this you should feel your palm becoming warm. When you feel ready, say the following words three times:

Lady Luck
shine on me
Help me with the lottery.
I am not starved,
I am not greedy,
Bring me luck when
I am needy.

When you buy your next lottery ticket, wrap it round the four-leafed clover until it is time to check your numbers. If you are using your lucky clover for a competition, place the charm on top of the entry while you fill out your name and address. And always carry your four-leafed clover in your purse or wallet at other times.

If you haven't used your lucky charm for a while, recharge it by repeating the incantation three times.

Did you know?

The Druids were the first to believe in the power of the four-leafed clover. The pretty little weed is in fact a freak of nature – the more common type being the three-leafed variety. Only about one in every ten thousand three-leafed clover have the extra leaf – so you will be very lucky to find it.

MONEY, MONEY, MONEY

The universe provides us with what we need – and that includes sufficient money for our needs. But if you find that you have more bills than salary, try this little money luck spell. Remember: all spells work best when there is a genuine need, so don't be greedy or do this spell just for the sake of it. If you really need some extra cash, this spell will work.

YOU WILL NEED:

A note of your own currency

One green candle

Five peppermint leaves

Five silver coins

Some salt water (two teaspoons of salt to 50 ml (2fl oz) of water)

Matches or a lighter

A cup of boiled water

WHAT YOU DO:

You should do this spell on a Friday or a full moon. First of all, place the paper money under your green candle. (If you really are that broke that you don't have a note, don't worry – you can always raid the Monopoly set, or even draw your own money.) Arrange the five peppermint leaves round the base of the candle in a circle. Next, wash the silver coins in the salt water to cleanse any negativity from them, and then place one coin on top of each peppermint leaf. Light the candle, and say the following words five times:

Oh Money Lord
Hear my plea
Send some money
on to me.
Look my way,
look my way
Hear my plea and
brighten my day.
Thank you, so mote it be.

Allow the candle to burn down. Then, take the mint leaves and place them in a cup of boiled water, allowing them to brew for five minutes. Take the leaves out and sip the peppermint tea. The leaves will have absorbed the magick that you put into them, and will in turn be absorbed back into you.

Keep the coins in your purse or wallet along with the note that you placed under the candle. Allow the mint leaves to dry out, then crush them and throw them out of the window. This signifies that the spell is complete.

REVERSE YOUR
LUCK

This is a ritual for when you feel as though the whole world is against you – it's probably not, but it may feel like that sometimes. If you think you need a complete change of luck in every area of your life, try this powerful candle spell.

YOU WILL NEED:

One long green candle

A silver pin

A green ballpoint pen

Matches or a lighter

WHAT YOU DO:

Start this spell on a Friday, ideally when the moon is full. Sometimes you might have to wait a full 29 days in order to do this spell on a full moon. If you can't wait for the full moon, don't worry too much – you should see the same results – but do try to start the spell on a Friday night.

You must keep this spell going for nine days in total for it to have its full effect, so leave your candle in a safe place where it won't be disturbed. First of all, divide the candle into nine equal parts by marking a horizontal line with the silver pin eight times down the stem of the candle. There should be about 2.5 cm (1") between each line, but obviously this depends on the size of your candle.

After doing this, close your eyes and stick the pin into the candle. It doesn't matter where – that's up to you. Next take your green pen and inscribe the word 'Luck' in each of the nine segments you have created. Ideally, on the first night of the full moon, leave your inscribed candle out in the garden or on a windowsill so that it catches full moonlight for one whole night. The following night, light the candle and say the following words six times:

Lord and Lady,
hear my plea
Make my fortune
change for me.
Banish now my
past misfortune
And return good luck
this full moon.

Allow the first segment of the candle to burn down and then blow it out. Bow to the moon three times.

Repeat this process for the next eight nights. When the pin falls from the candle, this is the sign that your bad luck has ended. If you have any wax left after the nine days, bury it in your garden. You should soon notice an improvement in your luck.

TURN LOVE AROUND

We've all had a run of bad luck when it comes
to affairs of the heart. If you notice that
you keep attracting unsuitable partners or
your relationships don't work out, it might be
because you're giving out the wrong signals –
signals saying that you don't care how you're
treated. If so, try this little spell to fix
matters for ever and banish bad luck from
your love life.

YOU WILL NEED:

One sheet of black
paper

Scissors

One sheet of pink paper

One black candle

Five pins

Matches or a lighter

WHAT YOU DO:

Do this spell on a waning moon. First of all, cut
five small heart shapes out of the black paper –
these represent the bad luck you've experienced
in your past love life. (It doesn't matter if
you're not very crafty and your paper hearts
don't come out looking like they ought to. A tip:
if you fold a piece of paper in two and then cut
half a heart shape out, it's easier than trying
to create a symmetrical heart freehand.)

Next, cut five larger heart shapes out of
the pink paper – these represent the new good
luck that you will have in your love life in
the future (the important part is that they
are larger than the black hearts).

Before you light your black candle,
inscribe it with the word 'Banish' using one of
the pins. Light the candle and then wrap one
pink heart around one black heart. Pin both

hearts together securely, so that the pink one completely encloses the black one, which can't escape. Chant the following as you do this:

By the power of love
And the Goddess above
Banish this bad luck
And make me lucky in love.

When you have pinned all five pairs of hearts, leave them out while the candle burns down. This spell will banish the attraction of bad luck in love and send signals out to the universe that you wish to invite only good partners into your life from now on.

When the candle has burned down, take the five pinned hearts and bury them in your garden or in a flower pot in your home. Soon, the paper will rot away in the soil and, as it does so, your bad luck in love will go away.

MIND, BODY AND SPIRIT

The original wise women were strong women, dedicated to healing and understanding the power of the earth, the sun and moon and the universe around us. In the twenty-first century, we have become disconnected with the power of nature and the ability to listen to our bodies. Part of modern witchcraft is to learn how to harness these powers for self-empowerment, and one of the positives of practising magick is to learn ways to increase our personal energies and spirit. Witches are natural healers and know how to listen to their body and the world around them.

CELEBRATE THE SEASONS

Just because most of us live in cities these days doesn't mean that we can't find ways to connect with the earth and the changing seasons, and their representations of life, death and rebirth. The seasons are ruled by the sun, which is symbolised by a wheel, and the moon turning around the sun is also a wheel, hence the Wheel of the Year. Note the eight wiccan sabbats and use these times to celebrate with others through ritual and connecting with nature, or make a sacred place or shrine at home to the Goddess and use a water purification for cleansing.

EMBRACE NATURAL REMEDIES

You don't need a huge garden or expensive organic grocery store on your doorstep to find healing through herbs and plants. Simple steps such as hanging sprigs of healing herbs (such as sage or lavender) in your home or car will influence your own energies and those of the people around you.

LISTEN TO YOUR BODY

It's easy to think of your body as something separate from yourself – something that you take for granted and then get annoyed at if it starts to go wrong. Take some time to learn to listen to your body. It may be through mindfulness or meditation, perhaps hiking in nature, or stretching yourself with mountaineering or extreme sports. Learn to understand the different ways your body informs who you are. Stress is a way in which the modern world interrupts our own magickal abilities and insights, making it harder for you to make the best decisions about your life or by making you susceptible to unkind influences. By taking ownership of your body and health, you are a small step closer to greater happiness and success.

BE THANKFUL

It is so empowering to embrace who you are and be grateful for your strengths and acknowledge your weaknesses. Why not create a self-care ritual once a week or month. Find a quiet time and place some symbols of who you are proud to be in front of a candle. Use your senses to take a few moments to think about how great you are and what you want to achieve in the next week or month. Let yourself be guided by your own body rather than external voices and messages.

It should be noted that witchcraft and spell-crafting is never an alternative to medical advice, so if you don't feel well then do talk to your doctor or medical advisor.

A HAPPY LIFETIME

CHARM

This uplifting spell is for a bride-to-be, to be performed the night before your wedding to bring you luck in love with your partner for the future. These ingredients represent all you need for a successful marriage – the lavender signifies good health, the mint leaves are for prosperity, the allspice represents a spiced-up love life, and the red rose petals the strong love between you and your partner.

YOU WILL NEED:

A handful of lavender

A handful of mint leaves

A handful of allspice

Two red rose petals

A rectangle of pink fabric 15 x 10cm (6 x 4")

One metre (one yard) of pink ribbon

Two drops of lavender oil

WHAT YOU DO:

Mix all the ingredients together in a small bowl. As you stir them together say the following words:

> *This magick mix will bring magick to our marriage.*
> *This magick mix will bring happiness, laughter and love for evermore.*

Now, with the fabric make a small pouch to hold your magick mix. Fold the material in two, short sides together, to form a 7.5 x 10 cm (3 x 4") rectangle, and sew up the open long side and one of the shorter sides to form a pocket. Fill the pocket with your magick mix and tie the top together with the piece of pink ribbon.

On the eve of your wedding day, place the pouch under your pillow. The lavender alone will help you to sleep well and absorb any negative thoughts or worries you may have for the following day.

On the morning of your wedding, drop two drops of lavender oil into a basin of warm water and wash your face. Make sure that when you leave your home for the wedding you take your magick pouch with you. Place it somewhere only you know where it is – in your flowers, your bag, or attached to the inside of your dress. You are guaranteed to have a wonderful wedding day and a blissful marriage.

Did you know?

We all know that a horseshoe is supposed to be lucky, but do you know why? The U-shape of the horseshoe is the most powerful sign of protection, and any bad luck thrown to a U-shape will simply rebound to the original source. Also, a horseshoe is nailed with seven nails, and seven is one of the luckiest numbers around. To receive luck from a horseshoe, it must be found, not purchased. And, according to the Greeks and Romans, the horseshoe should be placed over a doorway.

LOOKING FOR LUCK

It would be impossible for me to think of every
situation where you might need a good luck spell,
but I have tried to cover most eventualities.
However, if I haven't touched upon a specific
situation for which you need some extra luck, try
this spell which works for most things.

YOU WILL NEED:

Either the seed from
a thistle bush or a
white feather

WHAT YOU DO:

You can perform this spell at any time you like.
In England where I live, there is a lovely
thistle bush that produces small, white fluffy
seeds that blow through the air during the
summer. Traditional folklore says that these
are nature's fairies, sent to grant us wishes.
It is said that if you manage to catch one and
whisper your wish to it, then let it go, your wish
will be granted. If you are lucky enough to find
one of these thistle seeds, catch it, close your
eyes and make your lucky wish.

If you don't have one of these little fairies,
you can do exactly the same with a white
feather. Make your wish to it, then blow it into
the universe and your wish will soon come true.

BANISH BAD LUCK

This is one of those wonderfully versatile spells that you can do to banish any form of bad luck you may have experienced – whether you've lost your job, lost the love of your life, had bad luck in money or just feel like things are always going wrong. Try this spell to put a halt to all that bad luck.

YOU WILL NEED:

A silver pen

- -

A piece of black paper

- -

One black feather

- -

One back envelope

- -

Matches or a lighter

- -

A heatproof dish

- -

WHAT YOU DO:

Do this spell on a new moon. Using the silver pen on the black paper, write down the details of whatever bad luck has entered your life, and that you wish to be banished forever. Write it as though you are writing a letter to Mr Bad Luck and let him know in no uncertain terms that you won't tolerate any more bad luck in your life. Get angry if you want to, and let all your feelings pour out – but don't let Mr Bad Luck bring you down. You're telling him how it is, not the other way around.

Place the black feather with the letter in the envelope and seal it. Take the envelope outside and set fire to it in the heatproof dish, This will destroy any bad luck that has been sent to you so that you can start afresh and look forward to the good luck about to come your way.

CONFIDENCE
CHARM

We all need a boost sometimes when we'd rather hide under the duvet than face the day. Whether you've been unlucky in something important to you or are just struggling to find your mojo, this lovely charm is sure to boost your confidence and put a smile back on your face.

YOU WILL NEED:

A small, empty powder compact with a mirror inside

- -

A piece of paper cut in a circle to fit inside the compact

- -

Glue

- -

A pen with gold or silver ink

- -

WHAT YOU DO:

Do this spell on a Sunday when there is a new moon. First, get dressed in a favourite outfit, brush your hair, put on some makeup if you want to and generally make yourself feel good. Have a long soak in the bath if you want or just spend a bit of time pampering yourself in peace.

When you're feeling happy and relaxed, sit down and write on your circle of paper – in gold or silver ink – all the positive things you can think of about yourself. Remember the positive things other people have said to you and think of the times when you felt most confident. What was it that attracted your partner or your ex or your friends to you? How many times have you been told how lovely your smile is or how caring you are? If you really can't think of anything, phone a friend and ask them to tell you five of your positive qualities off the top of his or her head and write them down.

Glue the piece of paper inside your compact where the powder used to be. Now, look in the compact's mirror and see how special you really are. Say six times:

I am a wonderful and confident person now.

Keep your compact in your bag and every time you need a quick confidence boost, open the compact, read your note to yourself, and smile. You will feel 100 percent better every time.

Did you know?

The poor black cat has a lot to answer for. In many cultures around the world, it's tipped to be variously a good or bad omen. In the UK, it is supposedly lucky to see a black cat. It's the same in Germany, but the cat must cross your path from left to right. In other countries, a black cat crossing your path indicates imminent death, but in Scotland, a black cat arriving at a house indicates prosperity.

BANISH A SPECIFIC BAD LUCK

There might be a specific area of your life where you have had a run of bad luck, and which I haven't covered in this book. You can adapt most spells to suit your own situation, but if there is a subject that I haven't touched upon, this spell is designed to cover every kind of bad luck.

YOU WILL NEED:

A piece of paper

A pen

One black candle

Matches or a lighter

A heatproof dish

WHAT YOU DO:

Do this spell on a waning or new (dark) moon. First and foremost, concentrate on the situation from which you wish to banish bad luck. Write it down on the piece of paper. Write as much as you can about the situation – it could be that you feel your career, or your ability to find the right partner or the home of your dreams, is plagued by bad luck.

If so, write it down, including as much or as little detail as you like. Light the black candle, and say the following words:

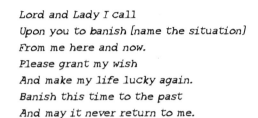

Lord and Lady I call
Upon you to banish [name the situation]
From me here and now.
Please grant my wish
And make my life lucky again.
Banish this time to the past
And may it never return to me.

When the candle has burned halfway down, set
fire to the piece of paper and drop it into the
heatproof dish. Carry the ashes outside and
allow the wind to take them away.

   Imagine your worries being swept away with
the wind – never again to return.

DREAMBOARD OF FORTUNE

This is a great thing to do on your own, or gather a few friends round and make a fun night of it. Either way, make your dreamboard on a new moon or a full moon.

YOU WILL NEED:

A large piece of card in your favourite colour

Coloured pens

Sticky stars

Glitter in different colours

Pressed flowers or potpourri

Glue

A selection of magazines or tear-outs of things that inspire and attract you

----

WHAT YOU DO:

First of all, place the piece of card on the floor in front of you and think of it as a clean sheet. As from now on, this is going to be the new you. Forget about any problems from the past. The past is the past. Forget about the trouble you had getting through your last exam, or the arguments with your parents, or getting into debt and so on. This is your brand new start.

Next, write on your piece of card in big letters 'My Dreamboard – Where Wishes Come True' across the top of the card. You can decorate this title with stars, glitter, pressed flowers, feathers, or whatever you want. The most important thing with your dreamboard is to make sure the things you put on there are the things you want, not your parents' wishes, not your friends' ideas – yours. You'll find it easier to start off with small things to begin with, so think about something small that you want right now. A new pair of boots? OK, now look through the magazines and find a picture of what you want. Cut it out and stick it on your card. Next to the picture write something like, 'I can now afford to buy this new pair of boots.' This simple, positive statement is enough to make your dream of owning it soon become a reality.

Now, go on to something else you want in your life, say in a few months' time. It could be to have a better social life, or to be fitter and healthier. It could be that you want to pass your driving test or find more free time for a hobby. Whatever it is you want to achieve, cut out an image that represents your wish and stick it onto your dreamboard.

The purpose of the dreamboard is that you build up a series of your ideal life in picture form. Every time you see the images on your board or spend time decorating it, you will magickally kick your subconscious into believing that you deserve these things and, more importantly, it will give you the focus and positivity you need to achieve them. As your attitude begins to change, you will attract new opportunities – the right opportunities – so that you will in turn attract more money, time and connections to the things on your dreamboard and everything else you want in life happen.

WITCHY WISDOM

I sometimes get asked what to do if spells don't work.

Spells often surprise us by working in a totally different way than we expected, and sometimes it's not until we look back that we can see that the spell actually did work. Magick won't make everything you want just appear. Magick can, however, influence the world and empower you to create the life you want. What's more, once you begin to use the magick in your life as nature intended, other people will soon see a different, more confident you. Magick won't promote greediness and wanting more than you actually need.

Occasionally a spell may seem not to work. If this happens, don't despair. There is usually a reason why spells don't work. If you've just come out of a bad relationship and feel desperate to find another partner, the Goddess might think you need some time to yourself to really get over the one who broke your heart. You might not be ready to fall head over heels in love again just yet. You might have cast a spell to achieve your dream job, and failed to get past the first interview stage. What if it turned out to be a really horrible place to work? Or, it isn't really your ideal job, just what you've convinced yourself you need, and you would really prefer to travel the world for a year.

If you cast a spell and it really is what you desire, but it doesn't work, check that you're casting it in the right moon phase, or change the spell slightly. For example: say you want to do a spell to increase your finances, but the moon is in the waning (banishing) phase. Change the words in your spell from attracting money, to banishing money worries. If you still have no success, then consider if your desire really is what is good for you or the person you're casting it for.

Magick really does give you the power to create your best life, so I hope that these spells are the start of a new and exciting time in your life, and the beginning of your understanding of witchcraft.

Merry Meet, Merry Part,
and Merry Meet Again.

An Hachette UK Company
www.hachette.co.uk

First published in the UK in 2018 by ILEX,
a division of Octopus Publishing Group Ltd
Octopus Publishing Group
Carmelite House, 50 Victoria Embankment
London EC4Y 0DZ
www.octopusbooks.co.uk
www.octopusbooksusa.com

Design, layout and text copyright
© Octopus Publishing Group Ltd 2018

Distributed in the US by Hachette Book Group
1290 Avenue of the Americas, 4th and 5th Floors,
New York NY 10104

Distributed in Canada by Canadian Manda Group
664 Annette St., Toronto, Ontario, Canada M6S 2C8

Editorial Director: Helen Rochester
Commissioning Editor: Zara Anvari
Managing Editor: Frank Gallaugher
Senior Editor: Rachel Silverlight
Publishing Assistant: Stephanie Hetherington
Art Director: Julie Weir
Designer: Louise Evans
Production Controller: Grace O'Byrne

ISBN 978-1-78157-622-9

A CIP catalogue record for this book
is available from the British Library.

Printed and bound in China

Picture acknowledgements:
Dreamstime.com: Cover art work by Julia Tochilina and Olgers1; Andrey Yanushkov 7, 8-9, 19,
66al, 66ar, 66bl, 69, 73, 102, 137, 141; Anna Maslikova 123; Artur Ganiev 45, 129; Arxichtu4ki 96a;
Astro Ann 14; Cmwatercolors 113; Daria Timofeeva 38a; Daria Ustiugova 83, 124; Dmitry Krikun 63;
Dvoriankin 116; Ekaterina Arkhangelskaia 27, 50b; Ekaterina Arkhangelskaia 130; Ekaterina
Glazovak 86; Elena Medvedeva 142; Evgenia Silaeva 88; Inna Sinanova 109; Kotokomi 10; Krystsina
Kvilis 4, 36, 65; Lemaris 46; Lnsdes 22, 66br, 139; Matikaby 71, 79r; Natali Myasnikova 91; Nattle
106; Oksana Adigamova 50a; Olgers1 30; Regina Jersova 56, 791; Shliago 133; Suandokdesign 33;
Svetlana Foote 2; Svitanola 105a; Tatiana Satarikova 41; Tetiana Syrytsyna 59, 96b; Tetiana
Syrytsyna 127; Transfuchsian 35; Undrey 38b; Victoria Arefyeva 56; Viktorkashin10 114;
Yuliya Derbisheva 74; Yunaco 23; Zeninaasya 80; Zeninaasya 105b.